For Black Writers...

For Black Writers...
A Personal Account of How to Write, Publish & Market
Your First Book
By Aliona L. Gibson
Copyright 1996
A.L.G. Publishing

Published by A.L.G. Publishing, 2625 Alcatraz Avenue, Suite #169, Berkeley, CA 94705

Original cover design: Monica Friedlander
Text & cover design: Cedric Brown

ISBN #: 0-9662654-0-8
Library of Congress Catalog Card Number: 98-91191

Printed in the USA by

MORRIS PUBLISHING

3212 East Highway 30 • Kearney, NE 68847 • 1-800-650-7888

For Black Writers...

A Personal Account of How to Write, Publish & Market Your First Book

by
Aliona L. Gibson

author of
Nappy: Growing Up Black & Female in America

This book is dedicated to
the memory of
my paternal grandmother
Eloise Avis Gibson
"Ma"
(1926-1996)
whose love and compassion
will inspire me always.

CONTENTS

- Black Literary Agents
- Black Publishing Companies
- Books/Periodicals/Articles
- Distribution Companies
- Online/Internet Resources
- Organizations & Agencies
- Writing Workshops/Retreats/Conferences

For Black Writers...

Acknowledgements

I would like to give a most heartfelt and sincere thanks to everyone who bought a copy of *Nappy* and passed the word around about my book. And for those of you who took the time to write me letters (especially Terrence Barrett, Lisa "Nkenge" Neal, Nikki Wade and Lisa Sims), I am most grateful for your words of support and encouragement. They could not have come at better times.

To my wonderful, beautiful mother Earlene C. Sanders who heard me read from "Hair Peace" so much she should know it by heart. And my other mom Sharon Townsend, she was there too! And to all of my homegirls who met me in Chicago and helped pass out flyers at The Today's Black Woman Conference before the book even came out: Boo Peters, Felicia Verdin, Shirley Paschal and Zoe Adams. And my gurl Shiree Dyson for hooking up with the internet/online section of this book.

This book would still be sitting on my book shelf collecting dust if it were not for the following people, to whom I am eternally grateful: My editor Amy Smith who did about twenty times more work than I paid her for. Allison Philips for the proofreading and great conversations and Cedric Brown, (whose words "I can do the design and layout for your book" were music to my ears) for his incredible enthusiasm & creative energy. Thanks to Thembisa Mshaka for reading it and giving me feeback in the early stages. Dawit Taddese was as sweet as pie and hooked me up with the right printer cartridges and paper. Special thanks to Elaine Lee for helping me get the job where I earned the money to publish this book.

To everyone who shared their stories and allowed me to interview them for this book. Special thanks to my sister-writer-friends Monique Gilmore-Scott whose friendship is invaluable and Tina McElroy Ansa for being so wonderful and accessible. Nancy E. Johnson whose poetry moves me in a way that makes me wish I could write poems.

For listening and encouraging me: Rosalyn Coleman, Alison Fletcher, Reginald Hawkins, Dymilah Hewitt,"Lemo", Ragni Larsen, Monte Lawson, Lisa Manning, Ave Montague, Olufola Sababu, Ronald Turner, Evelyn C. White, Angela Winn, and anyone else who I may have inadvertently left out. I could go on and on, really, but since I'm paying for this book by the page I'll stop here!

Introduction

Writing and getting my book *Nappy: Growing Up Black & Female in America* published is one of my biggest personal accomplishments. I wrote it with the desire to "finish something that I started" for once in my life. The book went into a second printing and has sold nearly ten thousand copies. By New York, large-publishing-house standards that's not so great. According to my standards, which mean far more to me, it makes the book a great success! I knew absolutely nothing about the publishing industry and had published nothing more than "letters to the editor" in newspapers and magazines, two to be exact.

When I first started my book, I walked into my local Black bookstore and asked for anything that might help me. The only advice I was given was to "keep writing" -- which is great advice, but I was looking for something that would tell me how to get what I had written published!

The most important words of wisdom I can share with other writers is "the more you know the better off you are." The publishing industry is not unlike most others in this country: it's very easy to get taken, so the more knowledge you have the better off you will be. Most publishers are more concerned with making money than whether or not a deal is advantageous to you. Sure, it's an honor to be published, but contrary to what publishers believe, you should get more out of the deal than just seeing your book in print.

For Black Writers... is a prime example of the nature of the industry, I was told over and over by agents and publishers not to waste my time on this book. They were looking at it in terms of how much money it could make instead of whether there was a market for it or whether it could help people. This is a perfect example of how important it is to take matters into your own hands, like I did with getting *Nappy* published! If I listened to them, this book (or *Nappy*) would not exist.

This book is for writers who wish to take the more traditional route to getting published: finding an agent, as well as those who wish to take a more assertive, non-traditional, grassroots approach like I did. Either way, it's in your best interest to have some knowledge of the industry and be aware of your options. Fortunately, Doubleday and Random House are not the only way to go. One of my objectives with this book is to present those options as well as to inspire writers by sharing my story. I honestly believe that if I could do it, so can you!

This book is not meant to be the be-all, end-all book on getting published. There are tons of books on the market about how to do it (some of which are listed in the reference section of this book). *For Black Writers...* is the story of how I did it, a record of the road I travelled to getting published. With all of the books by Black authors being published, we should have more of a hand in the business aspect of the industry than we do. It amazes me that there are so few Black literary agents and publishers. If quality books for and by Black people are going to continue to be published, I believe it is imperative that we become more involved in the business side of things.

I have learned quite a bit in the past few years since starting my book and becoming an author; my intention with this book is to simply share those things. I hope that this book and my story will assist and inspire anyone who wishes to write and be published. Good Luck!

Aliona L. Gibson
November 1997

Section 1: Writing Your Book

A supermodel who had just come out with a novel once said in a magazine interview, "Actually I had someone else write the book, but I came up with the plot and characters." I couldn't believe she had the nerve to tell people that! Last time I checked, an author was defined as someone who wrote a book, not just came up with ideas for it. This section is intended to help people who want to actually write their own stories, not give the task to someone else to do.

The most important thing about writing is giving yourself permission to do it. Feeling that you have something to say, that your story is worthy of being told, is essential. I must admit, when I first started writing my book, for about a tenth of a second I wondered whether I should even do it. I thought "Who's going to want to read a book by a twenty five year-old?" Fortunately the thought left as quickly as it came. Being a writer means acknowledging the fact that you have a story to tell; that what you have to say is just as important as what anyone else has to say.

I had a story to tell, which would eventually become my book, *Nappy*.

My Story

Nappy was born out of my desire to write, not to actually write a book. Writing has always come sort of naturally for me. When I was in elementary school I enjoyed writing little stories. Then, in junior high school, I kept a diary. Like most people, I just wrote about whatever was on my mind at the time, whatever my issues were that particular week. Writing was an emotional outlet, plus I really enjoyed doing it.

I continued to write for myself for years before I finally decided to try my hand at getting something published. The first thing I submitted was an essay called "Hair Peace." Having recently had my hair cut into a short afro, I found the responses I was getting so interesting I decided to write about them--basically I gave the lowdown of the politics of hair in the Black community. After a few weeks re-writing the piece and getting feedback from my roomate at the time, it turned out to be what I thought was a well-written, funny and honest essay. Eagerly I sent it off to *Essence*, not thinking for a minute that they would reject it. Ah, youthfulness!

Well, they did reject it. But I enjoyed working on my essay so much I decided to do another one. At that time there was a Revlon television commercial featuring anorexic-looking models dancing to a pseudo house-music song, "Shake That Body." I saw this commercial over and over again and each time it infuriated me! Finally, out of disgust, I began to write about Black women and body image, specifically my own issues.

After that it seemed like I was consumed. Every time I thought of something to do an essay about and started writing, the idea for another one came up. So

I just wrote, with no intention of finishing the pieces in any order or all at one sitting. I wrote about all kinds of things: my trip to Africa, living in New York, college days, my family, mentors, etc. I bought several two-pocket folders, labeled one for each essay, and started carrying them around with me. Whenever I got the urge to write something down, I did. Then I would enter everything I'd written into my computer at work and carry the printouts with me. Again, it never felt like writing a book, just like getting some stuff off my chest. At some point it also became a personal challenge to finish something I had started (for once)!

One day I decided to print out all the essays at once. Right away away I noticed there was quite a bit of work and that it looked like a manuscript. That's when I decided to solicit what eventually became *Nappy* to publishers.

Telling Your Story

Everyone has a story to tell. It kills me to hear people say "I wish I could write but I just don't have what it takes". I hear it over and over, people feeling like nobody would want to read something they wrote or that it wouldn't be interesting. I feel like all of our stories, both real and imagined, are worthy of being told.

You don't have to be rich and famous to have had an interesting life or to feel like you have something of value to say. A great example is Maya Angelou: who told this poor little nappy-headed southern girl that her life and experiences would be worthy of a book? And who would have guessed that *I Know Why the Caged Bird Sings* would become a national bestseller?

What makes one story more interesting than another is the manner in which it is told. Your "story" doesn't mean only a memoir or autobiography either. Stories come in all forms and fashions, they are both those which are real and those that are imagined. They can be poems, songs -- some stories are told through the voice of a character in a novel. How many novels have you read and afterwards wondered if they were auto-biographical?

Try not to concern yourself with little details that might get in the way of getting the major writing done. For example, if your writing is flowing, don't stop because you can't think of a certain word, leave it blank and go back to it later. Just do the best you can, say everything you need to say, and as one of my favorite authors Jill Nelson inscribed in my copy of one of her books, "the universe will handle the details."

Fiction vs. Non Fiction
I have always been drawn to real life stories and expe-riences. That may be why most of what I write comes out of some experience that I have had or something I am particularly moved by.

Once I was bawled out by a well-known fiction writer who gave me a lecture about "real" writing. When I told her that writing nonfiction was what I felt most comfortable with, she went off on me. I don't remember all of what she said, but it included, "You have a brain—use it!" I left her not feeling very good about my writing. It wasn't until later that I realized I didn't have anything to feel bad about and that I should learn to accept advice graciously but do what works for me. If I feel good writing nonfiction, then that is what I need to do.

Everyone is entitled to whatever type of writing they choose. One of many helpful things I learned at a writing retreat is the phrase, "real or imagined." We need to realize that our stories, both real and imagined, are worthy of being told. Real or imagined, our stories count too!

In terms of getting published, as a first-time author you would be better off having at least the first draft of your novel or at the very least a good synopsis and the first three chapters. It shows people in the industry that you are serious and have more than just ideas to present to them. Nonfiction books require a book proposal, which I explain the contents of in Section 2 of this book. Having a good proposal shows an agent or prospective publisher that you've thought out your book and it will also help you visualize the contents. The chapter by chapter breakdown can be used to formulate the outline of your book.

The Writing Process
Everyone has a different approach to writing and what works for them. Mine, such as it is, is to just sit

down and start writing, either at my computer or on a yellow legal pad. Usually it's about something that's a "hot button" issue for me, so writing is a way of getting it off of my chest. I heard poet and author of *Keepin' It Real*, Kevin Powell say that writing is therapy for him.

Evelyn C. White, my writing mentor, said something once in a workshop I hadn't thought of before. She said that a whole bunch of things that are part of the writing process go on in your head before you actually sit down at your computer or with your pad and pen. I can definitely relate to that; I'm always tossing and churning ideas around in my head. I think so much about a project before starting to write, by the time I do it it's just a matter of getting it out of my head and onto the page.

Here are a few practical things that I try to keep in mind when I am writing:

Outlines
An "outline" is a skeleton of a book, a list of all the main ideas and points you wish to cover, in order. When you sit down to write you just fill it in.

An outline can make the task of writing a book less overwhelming. I didn't use an outline for *Nappy* because the more I wrote, the more the pieces became clear and I was able to visualize what I wanted them to be about. For the book I'm working on now I do need more structure and am finding an outline kind of hard to do. I'm used to being able to just sit down and start writing! In the long run though, I think the outline can be extremely helpful. Writing a book can seem like an overwhelming task so outlines can break it down in a way that makes it easier to tackle. A good place to start would be jotting down all of the main points and/or themes I want to address in the book.

Feedback

Sometimes you can get too close to your own work. Reading something you've written over and over can make it seem stale and hard to see with a critical eye. This is why letting other people read your work can be so important.

One of the things that kept me motivated to finish writing my manuscript was letting a few people read what I had written. I was shy and super selective about who I let read it. Dee, my coworker at the time, was the first. She was reading my essays well before it ever dawned on me to solicit them to publishers. She loved them and would always ask for the next one. She also proofread for me, which I appreciated.

At the same time, you should be careful about getting too many opinions or too much advice while you are writing. It can be confusing and conflicting so I suggest saving serious changes for the advice of a professional editor.

Rewriting, Rewriting, Rewriting

For some writers rewriting is the most important part

of the writing process. Often, giving your work a little time to "marinate" allows you to come up with more things to add to make the piece stronger.

Rewriting and professional editing made *Nappy* a major improvement over what I had initially written. I don't mind this part of the writing process because I know that the end result will be better than what I started out with. That doesn't mean that it always comes easily. Sometimes I find it hard to rewrite. It's almost like I am afraid of messing it up.

Another reason to get used to rewriting is that selling a manuscript doesn't mean the writing part is over. After being edited, you will probably be asked to expand certain areas, while others will be cut out.

Whenever you read a book or magazine article, you have no idea how many times what you're reading has been rewritten. You'd be surprised at how many times some writers rewrite their work. For *Nappy* I rewrote in sections, as opposed to trying to do the whole manuscript at once, which would have been overwhelming. Even after rewriting it several times on my own, it still turned out a lot stronger after the assistance of a professional editor. Once I get everything down, I go over it and either add more or take some out. Recently I've gotten into the habit of reading my work aloud and making changes from there.

Editing "Nappy"

After I signed the contract with Writers & Readers

they hooked me up with a young woman at another publishing house. I don't know what had been discussed about the shape of my manuscript between my publisher and this editor, only that she was going to help me clean it up and make it tighter. She suggested the book would be stronger with more anecdotes, dialogue and scene-setting. I made her suggested changes and sent her my reworked sections one at a time. She was very thorough and only once or twice did we disagree on what we thought would work best for the manuscript, just minor stuff.

After the first editor stopped working on my manuscript, Deborah Dyson, the associate publisher at Writers & Readers took over. She felt it needed to be more cohesive; more like a memoir and less like a collection of writings. Immediately I freaked out. I thought they were asking me to reconstruct the whole book! Once I calmed down and gave it more thought I realized how easily some of the chapters could be combined. I put all of the pieces that dealt with issues of self-image together, and did the same for the pieces on relationships. The remaining essays had to do with places, so they were combined too. It actually fell together rather nicely, thank God.

What I didn't like about combining essays was dropping the opening quotes I had carefully chosen to open each piece. For my essay on my trip to Africa I found one from Marcus Garvey about knowing where you are from in order to know where you are going. For the one comparing living in New York to

California and the disadvantages of integration I used a quote from Malcolm X about how adding cream to black coffee makes it weak. My favorite was "There is power in the bootay" by Phyllis Yvonne Stickney, which I used for my chapter on body image. Fortunately I wasn't stuck on the idea of a collection of personal essays or we would have had real problems. I trusted that my publisher knew more about what would make the work stronger and more appealing.

Patricia Allen was the last person to work on my manuscript. She did a great job of cleaning it up and making sure it still sounded like me. Patricia was persistent about getting me to expand on certain things in the book and only once did we have a disagreement. She felt that I should say more about my mother. I love my mother but didn't feel that the book was about our relationship and wasn't going to force myself to write about her. We ended up making a compromise.

I feel extremely lucky that my book turned out pretty close to the way I submitted it. This is one of the benefits of doing business with a small press who is more concerned with producing good books than making the New York Times bestseller list. They didn't try to take my idea and switch it around into something they felt was more marketable than what I had written.

Make Time For Writing

The most important thing I can say about making time for writing is that being able to write full time is a luxury. It shouldn't be, but it is. It's really hard when you work forty hours a week at a day job, to write a book. It can be done though. As I was once told, nothing worth having (or doing) comes easy.

I don't have any special days or times when I write. I don't even write every day. I keep a journal which I carry around at all times and write in whenever the mood strikes me. When working on a project, I carry a smaller notebook just for ideas.

I guess when you feel passionate about something you will get obsessed with it. What I remember the most about writing Nappy is how driven — almost obsessed — I became. I got up early in the morning to write before work and stayed up late to write at night. My weekends were devoted to working on my book. When I got a new job and access to a computer, I often stayed after work to work on it. I have heard novelists say they think of things about their characters at all hours of the day, from the shower in the morning to lying in bed at night.

Writer's Block

Getting stuck while writing is a horrible thing. It happens to me and I think it's out of fear. I worry that it's not going to be as good on paper as when I tell it to other people or that whoever is editing it will think it's bad. I noticed how much harder it was to write after I knew people were going to read my work than when I was just writing for myself.

When I get stuck I usually just stop and try to do

something else. It doesn't have to be writing, but sometimes a journal entry or working on another piece gets the writing juices flowing again.

Staying Motivated

Reading - This may sound basic, but it's important: Good writers read. Reading exposes you to different styles and techniques. When you read a book that you enjoyed, think about what you liked about the book, what worked and what didn't. Think about how you think the author incorporated those qualities into their work. I know for me, I like to feel some sort of connection with the writer. I think that happens when writers write from the heart and write their truth.

Read a variety of things and visit bookstores frequently to stay up on what is being published and by whom. That's how I knew that my book would be only one of three memoirs by those of us in the post-civil rights generation at that time (Sister Souljah's *No Disrespect* and Marcus Mabry's *White Bucks and Black-Eyed Peas* were the other two).

Journal Writing - I can undoubtedly say that my journal writing was an asset in getting me to conceptualize my first book. If I had not been an avid journal writer it would have been a lot harder to do.

I don't remember what made me start , but I kept a diary growing up. I do remember really enjoying making entries. It wasn't until I got older that I realized how therapeutic writing can be. The idea of witnessing personal growth didn't dawn on me until, like I said in the preface of *Nappy*, I found an old diary and was amazed at how much I had changed.

People always tell me they try to keep a journal but don't do it consistently. I believe you will write in your journal as much as you need to. Rarely do I write in my journal on a daily basis. Sometimes I write in it more than others. I feel like the more you do it, the more you will feel like you need to. In other words, it becomes habitual.

Courses and Writers Groups - I highly recommend that aspiring writers take writing courses. Since I want to be the best possible writer I can, I am planning to go to graduate school to afford myself the time to work on developing my craft. My sister-writer-friend Monique Gilmore had four novels out and took a writing course. There is always room for growth.

I don't belong to a writing group but I think it can be a great thing. Not only is it a supportive environment, it would give you a chance to share your work and ideas with others. Writing is lonely so being around other people who are on the same path as you can be a welcome change of pace. It can also be a time to break the monotony of working on a project. Since most groups have timed writing exercises, it can be your chance to write something other than that book you've been pecking away at!

When I get the time to work seriously on my novel

idea I am planning to take a course called "Creating Your Novel" which I think will help me tremendously. The course description promises that participants will have an outline and a few sample chapters of their idea by the end of the course.

Writing Retreats - Writing retreats offer a chance to get away from it all and concentrate exclusively on your writing (a real luxury for the majority of us!). Even full time, professional writers take part in retreats and colonies. They're revitalizing.

For my twenty-seventh birthday I treated myself to a women's writing retreat in Oregon called Flight of the Mind. After working full time in addition to working on my book, spending an entire week as a writer only was mighty enticing. Plus, I felt like I had been working hard and deserved it.

The workshop was productive and fun and worth every penny I scraped up to get there. It was held on the MacKenzie River, some miles outside of Eugene, so between classes there were hiking trails, hot springs and lakes to visit.

The classes themselves, in poetry, fiction, non-fiction and other specialties, met for a couple of hours each day. I took the non-fiction course with Evelyn C. White, which I found most gratifying. We were given sample articles to read and examine and read our work aloud in class. The class turned out to be more emotional than I had imagined, but things tend to get that way when you are dealing with telling the truth. To be among women of all ages and colors who shared a common thread was amazing.

I loved Flight of the Mind, but there are all kinds of worthwhile retreats and seminars out there. Some of them offer scholarships to writers who otherwise could not attend.

Persistence and Patience

The two most important qualities you can have as a writer trying to get published is to be patient and to be persistent. Getting published especially, being persistent is key. It takes persistence to actually finish a book too. I think of it this way: there are a lot of people out there who say they want to write a book, few actually start and even fewer of those actually finish. I know I want to be among those few who actually do it!

Persistence is important for anyone in this industry. Here's a good example: *Volunteer Slavery* (great memoir, by the way) was turned down by every major publisher in the country and was rejected over thirty times before it was picked up (by a Black house called The Noble Press which is listed in the reference section of this book). Jill Nelson's agent knew the importance of being persistent. When you believe in something, it's not hard. It can be discouraging but hanging in there is well worth the wait.

When I get told no, it's discouraging and I get depressed for a minute but then I use it as fuel to push me even harder to meet my goals. Between trying to get my articles published in magazines, trying to get an agent, publishers for my books, if I let being told no stop me, I wouldn't even be writing this book!

On being patient -- most agents take between four and six weeks to get back to you and editors at publishing houses take even longer. I literally count the days after I mail something off. I figure out when they are most likely to get it and proceed to count the number of weeks they have it for. I've learned that I should be writing while I am waiting. Writing a proposal for my next project or writing the next draft of whatever I am working on.

Protecting Your Work
When you do finish your manuscript the first thing you should do is send it out for a copyright. Do this before you submit it to agents or publishers. If you are extra paranoid about someone stealing your ideas, you should do it before letting anyone read the work in its entirety. The Library of Congress in Washington D.C. is the agency that does this service. It costs about $20 and the application process is really simple.

Another way to protect your work is to send a copy of your manuscript or synopsis to yourself by certified mail and then not to open it. The postmark will prove that your idea was just that — yours — on the date it was stamped. Sounds like an old wives' tale, but I did it and I still have it. To be safe though, I recommend paying the $20 to be sure your manuscript is legally protected. You'll also have the benefit of feeling "official."

Novelists

Because I would like this book to be useful to fiction as well as non-fiction writers, I've asked a couple of novelists I know to share their experiences and tricks of the trade. Monique Gilmore is a good friend and author of four books published by Arabesque, a line of African American romance novels. She will be making her debut in mainstream fiction with her tentatively titled novel *The Ties That Bind Way Down Deep*, which she completely finished before soliciting publishers. I'm still trying to figure out how Monique does it -- she's a writing whirlwind! I had the pleasure of meeting Tina McElroy Ansa a few years ago at an anniversary event for Oakland's oldest Black bookstore, Marcus Books. She is what I consider the quintessential novelist, and I hope what she has to share will prove to be as useful and inspiring for you as it was for me.

Monique Gilmore

Monique attributes the writing of her first book to Divine Intervention (Holy Spirit). "God takes care of fools, babies and new writers," she jokes.

Reading Terry McMillan's work helped Monique see that "regular people" who were good storytellers could become published writers. Intervention played a part because Monique had no idea what her story would be or what her characters would be like. She just sat down and started writing.

Several books later, Monique now understands how important an outline can be to a novel. "It's like building a house without a blueprint," she says. "If you don't have an outline and character sketches you will end up doing double work unnecessarily." The outline doesn't even have to be in complete sentences. "You may not even know all the parts at first and that's OK. Just write what you can."

Monique puts lots of work into her character sketches, taking extra time to think of names and creating her characters' lives for a clear picture to convey to her readers. She suggests coming up not only with physical characteristics but past histories as well. Historical events that occurred during the year your character was born, traumatic experiences and even who their first boy or girlfriend was are all details that can help develop a clear sense of character.

Figuring out why you want to write can help an aspiring writer. Monique suggests asking yourself, "Are you trying to change the way people view situations, draw compassion or share information?" Her first book, *No Ordinary Love*, was intended to enlighten female readers about the need to include blue collar men in their search for a mate. Her second, *Hearts Afire*, was an attempt to share a bit of the Black experience and to show the strong influence of grandmothers in our community. With *The Grass Ain't Greener*, Monique hoped to share information on the woes of married life in the '90s. Her fourth book, *Soul Deep*, is about the dangers of getting caught up in the

L.A. lifestyle of stardom, wealth and materialism. Monique is so adamant about the "just do it" philosophy of writing that she discourages new writers from taking part in writing groups and seminars. "You need to be writing," she stresses, recommending that you get the writing done first and then put it out there for feedback and opinions.

The biggest obstacle Monique faces as a writer is a common one: finding the time to write. Working full time leaves her an average of thirteen to sixteen hours per week in which to write, so she does it any place and time she can; during her lunch hour, under the hair dryer at the salon and before she goes to bed at night. When asked how she stays motivated, Monique says that seeing it through is where you are truly tested. Not just in writing but in anything you do in life. She feels that her drive and ambition are fueled by her desire to write and by her hunger for success as an author. "Once you finish the first one," she says, "it becomes easier and you are better able to see the light at the end of the tunnel."

Tina McElroy Ansa

I had the pleasure of meeting Tina McElroy Ansa a few years ago at an anniversary celebration event for Oakland's oldest Black bookseller, Marcus Bookstore (see "The Importance of Networking" in Section 3 of this book...). She so graciously agreed to speak with me about writing novels and her process. I hope what she has to share will prove to be as useful and inspiring for you as it was for me.

As I said before, Tina McElroy Ansa, in my opinion, is the quintessential novelist. Her books include *Baby of the Family* (1989), *Ugly Ways* (1993) and *The Hand I Fan With* (1996). She writes from her heart and soul as opposed to what the hot topic of the moment happens to be. Her books are well-crafted works of literary art which are graced with both substance and depth. She has mastered the art of storytelling, her work is steeped in the African American oral traditions.

Good novels have longevity. Tina's books are timeless and not trendy like a lot of the popular contemporary novels by African Americans on the market. That explains why her second novel *Ugly Ways* remained on the Essence Blackboard Bestseller list for two years!!

The first thing Tina said about being a writer is asking yourself a few questions: "Am I a writer?" "Am I ready to write whether or not I get published?" "Do I take myself seriously as a writer?" For her, these are very important questions. They will determine how serious you are about your writing and how much of a commitment you are willing to make to your craft, which is an essential part of being a writer and writing books.

For a novelist, ideas are in abundance. They should be coming from everywhere and if not, then you need to really think about whether or not novels are what you are supposed to be writing. If ideas are not in abundance then you are probably not allowing yourself to recognize ideas and you need to think about how you are looking at things. Most people lead busy, hectic lifestyles that prevent them from having enough quiet time or "thinking time" as she calls it. It's a time where you take notice of what's going on in the world, where you slow down and be quiet and listen to what is being said. Tina spends most of her quiet time in her garden but when and how you spend your quiet thinking time will vary from person to person.

She considers post-it notes one of the best inventions ever, using them to jot down ideas the immediate moment they enter her head. Once you write it down then you have to commit to finishing it. Ideas are important and writing them down is even more important since they don't count if they are in your head! Writing it down allows you to turn it loose so you can start expanding and moving on it. Ideas are like seeds or kernels which need to be nurtured in order to reproduce. Treat your ideas with respect by writing them down, it says "I am a writer, I have something to say."

On character development, Tina says you need to acknowledge envisioning your characters from the very start. Bits and pieces will come to you at various moments in time. You need to remember that as the writer you know what the character looks like and how she feels but you need to convey those ideas to your reader. If you don't how else will they know? These ideas are more seeds and kernels with which to work. You need to be able to share the intimate details of not only what your characters look like but also what they feel, what they think and what is in their past. Even if this information never appears in your actual manuscript it is important information which will help make the characters more clear to you.

Though she has never been a traditional outline kind of writer, she does use what she calls a working framework. It maps out the beginning, middle and end of a project. After that you will need to create more background information on your characters with intimate details such as what kinds of clothes they wear, do they wear make up or not, who was the first boy they kissed, do they have money, etc. You have to know your characters better than anybody. Knowing your characters and going into their backgrounds will give them inner life. These details will once again serve as seeds and kernels which will require your work and nurturing to prosper and grow. Details are the "gold" of her work, it's what she grew up with, the way people around her spoke.

Writing is an organic, very natural process to Tina. She shared with me a quote she liked and used in regard to the writing process. "No cheap tricks". That means that you cannot expect to go straight from A to M, taking shortcuts makes you short change yourself. If you make the commitment to being a writer, you will realize that you deserve more than being short changed. Writing is a process and needs to be respected. No cheap tricks means going from A to M, the organic way, A, B, C, D,........etc.

When she has a work in progress she writes daily. Once you make the commitment to yourself as a writer, discipline will not be a problem. Making that commitment means writing rather than watching talk shows, going to the movies or even out to dinner. Tina keeps a journal and tries to write in it a little everyday but sometimes the woes of daily life get in the way. Her usual routine includes writing everyday, weekends included. She wakes up at around seven a.m. and spends the first hour awake as her quiet time in which she meditates. She also spends a few hours in her garden where she thinks and reflects and works up a sweat! By eleven a.m. she is ready to shower, eat and start working. She sits at the computer until it's dark, stops to eat then goes back to her writing. Sometimes she stays up through the night writing. Personally, I could not think of a better way to spend a day!

Tina refuses to give the idea of writer's block any power. She is quick to dismiss it as a myth. She doesn't believe that it exists — if what you are working on doesn't wake you up with new ideas, maybe it is not ready to be written. If it doesn't work, it will work badly if you push it. Take it as a sign and go another way. Take time to start something else, write a poem, take time to think.

In a few words to writers of color, she says the most important thing we can do is realize how far ahead of the game we are. We come from a tradition that respects the word. Realize that your biggest gift as a writer to the world is who you are.

For Black Writers...

38

Section 2: Getting Your Book Published

I believe one reason my book was published at all is that it was ninety percent finished by the time I started soliciting publishers. I knew that it wasn't really "done" (is it ever?), but I had an actual manuscript to send if someone wanted to see my work.

You can't expect a publisher to give you money or want to publish your work on the basis of a good idea, especially if you are a first-time author like I was and had published nothing more than letters to the editor in newspapers and magazines. People want to see what you've actually done, not how many great ideas you have! I cannot stress enough the importance of actually finishing your work before trying to sell it. Being ready when my golden opportunity presented itself was the best thing I could have done.

I didn't know anything about publishing when I started soliciting my manuscript. Had I known more about the industry and how it works, I would have tried to get an agent first. But I decided, for the heck of it, to approach publishers myself. I really didn't think I would have any luck, and if I did, it would only be after submitting to hundreds and hundreds of publishing houses. As far as I was concerned, there was nothing to lose but the cost of the stamps.

Getting Started

Whenever you need information on something you know absolutely nothing about, a good place to start is your local library. So that's what I did. I went to the Berkeley Public Library's reference room and asked for a book on publishers. The woman at the desk handed me a large reference book called *The Literary Marketplace*. Because it couldn't be checked out, I took the book, some scratch paper and those little pencils they give you and sat at a table and copied the names and addresses of potential publishers.

The book listed publishing houses in alphabetical order and gave vital statistics for each one, like the managing editor's name, their address, fax number, number of books published each year, date they were founded, etc. I didn't know where to start, so I just began at the beginning: with the A's, blindly picking names and taking the addresses down. Since I was writing longhand, it took two or three trips to the library before I got my contract. I ended up submitting my manuscript to Writers & Readers Publishing, the company that eventually published *Nappy*, because I got bored going from the front of the book and decided to switch to the back, completely ignoring the x, y and z pages.

The Literary Marketplace
Recently I made a trip back to the Berkeley Public Library, to the same reference room where I had wandered in looking for a book on publishers several years before. I asked for *The Literary Marketplace* and realized for the first time how huge it was. I thought to myself, I must have been on a serious mission to have gone through this thing -- the book is over two

thousand pages long!! Still, I have declared this book the Bible of Publishing. It contains everything you would ever want to know on the subject and is a great place to start in trying to learn more about the business. In addition to information on getting your book published, it has a ton of resources that will be helpful in promoting it, such as radio and television stations with book-related shows. The book also lists book-related contests, awards, organizations and magazines. For people who wish to self-publish, the LMP includes book manufacturers, sales and distribution companies and an industry "yellow pages."

There are a lot of books available on all different aspects of the publishing industry, but I think *The Literary Marketplace* is the most comprehensive. You could probably use this one book and get all the information you need to publish and promote your book. (I did.)

My Query Letter

A query letter is your first chance to let potential publishers know how great an idea your book is. This will be their first impression of you, so you'll want it to be good. After reading your query letter a publisher should be dying to see more. You need to give them a sense of why you feel qualified to write about what you are proposing and why you think it's a great idea.

I have always been one to do things a little differently from the norm or from everybody else, and I used this philosophy when writing my query letter. I wanted my letter to give the reader a real sense of what I was about and what my book would be like: open, honest and very candid.

I needed something that would grab the attention of a person who reads hundreds and hundreds of query letters, so I ended up writing a letter about Black women and our "attitude problem." My first line was, "I know you've heard of it, and you have probably even experienced it yourself." After that I wrote very confidently about how my book would provide insight as to why some Black women are perceived as having an "attitude." Basically it laid the groundwork for the synopsis, which gave more details about the book itself. This is also your chance to introduce your "book hook", the thing that makes your book unique and different from anything else on the market.

I may have shocked a bunch of folks for having the guts to write such a letter, but like I said before, I felt there was nothing to lose. Not only that, I thought it was a great letter! You can see it along with the original synopsis in this book's Sample of Materials section.

Synopsis

Most agents and editors complain about getting too much stuff and not having enough time to read all of it. The best way to send information on your book is to send a synopsis.

My synopsis (a summary of sorts) was short and sweet; two pages. I don't know how I knew to do this; it's not like I had ever seen one before. It was just a few sentences on what each chapter was about, written in the same style that my cover letter and the book were: real, heartfelt and to the point.

As a visual aid I pasted a copy of one of my favorite photos of myself to the first page, hoping to grab someone's attention, I guess. Depending on the topic of your book a visual aid might not be necessary. If my book had been about anything other than issues of self-image and identity, I don't think I would have used a picture with it.

Your synopsis, just like your letter, should be neat and free of misspelled words or grammatical errors. I've heard over and over that nothing turns people in the publishing industry off more than these kinds of mistakes. In fact, anything you send out should always be typed (on computer is best), double spaced and with page numbers. It should always look neat and professional.

Book Proposal

In my long and exhausting effort to find the right agent, I came across a well-known high powered New York agent who was interested in seeing my work. When I told her I was using a book to write the proposal for my next book she said I didn't need an entire book and proceeded to fax me a three-page document explaining how to do a proposal. She told me that for nonfiction books agents use an authors proposal to sell books to prospective publishers. The author doesn't have to actually finish the book to get an advance. For fiction, first-time authors need to have a completed manuscript as well as a synopsis. First-time authors in particular need to show that you are serious. Like I said earlier, a lot of people say they want to write a book, few actually start and even fewer of those ever actually finish the book. Publishers and agents know this all too well so a first time author who has a completed manuscript will most likely get the attention of a prospective agent and/or publisher.

I found writing the proposal harder than writing my book! I guess it makes sense because you are trying to say in twenty or thirty pages what a two hundred and fifty page book is about! Your proposal should be well thought out and concise. Just imagine someone taking this document to someone and trying to convince them to give you a lot of money based on the quality of the document. This is what they will use to get you money and convince someone that it is worthy of being a book so you want to make it as good as you can.

I have listed a book in the reference section on writing your proposal which is helpful but here are the basic elements of a good proposal:

Introduction - The introduction is to explain what your book is about and why you are writing it. Also, why you feel there is a need for this particular book in the marketplace. This section will be an example of your writing capablities and your style. It can range from five to ten pages, maybe more or less depending on the type of book you are doing. The introduction for my second memoir was about ten pages.

Audience/Market - You need to convince folks that people will buy your book, that there is a market for it. Be as specific as possible. Include any statistics if you can, the more convincing the better.

Competitive & Comparative Titles - This involves staying up on what's being published and by whom. You need to know what's out there so you can tell them how yours is different. And if there is no book like the one you are proposing, put that in there!! If there are books similar to yours on the market you will need to examine (read) them and tell how yours is different, better.

Author biography - I talk about this in section three on "Promoting Your Book". In addition to being included in a press packet, your bio should be a detailed description of why you are qualified to write this book. Don't be shy about boasting on yourself. Be sure to include any seminars and appearances that are related to your book or area of expertise.

Chapter by Chapter breakdown - In order to show that you have the book well thought out and to let them know (in more detail than the intro.) what the book is about you will need to do a breakdown of each chapter or section. You should spend at least one page for each chapter, the more the better though. Like the rest of the proposal, it should be strong and convincing.

Book Format - This section, probably the shortest, depending on the type of book you are proposing, will give the logistics of the book: approximate word count, number of pages and/or photos and illustrations to be used. I talked about what I envisioned my cover to look like, although like I said later in the book, the author has very little to do with that part of the book, the first one anyway. It's good to show that you have given it thought.

Author Promotion - This section should tell the prospective publisher how you plan to promote your book once it is published. They will love to see this since most authors think they don't have to be involved in this part of the publishing process. Getting involved in promoting your book will let them know just how serious you are about your book doing well. It is ridiculous to leave it entirely up to the publisher. Section three of this book will give you what you need to write this seciton of your proposal.

Just like any and everything you send out, your proposal should be error free (please spell check!), double-spaced, numbered and I prefer laser printed with justified margins. I think it looks neater and more professional.

Putting it Out There

I sent my synopsis and cover letter out in groups of twenty. Twenty happened to be the number of stamps in a booklet, so I sent batches out as often as I could afford to buy one. I started receiving rejection letters, but not as many as the number of queries I sent out. Some people didn't even bother to respond to me. Others sent my query letter and synopsis back. One letter I received was in French -- I knew it was bad news because the only word I recognized was "regrets." Even so, I was still excited about sending my letters out and getting any kind of response at all.

Sixty or seventy letters later I started getting positive responses. Three, to be exact. The first positive response was from Doubleday Publishing. I was ecstatic! Visions of quitting my job, being able to write full time and book tours danced in my head. To me, Doubleday was the big leagues. The associate editor who responded wrote that if my stories were as good as my title then I was on to something. I sent her a note and my manuscript the next day.

Within a week I received an Airborne Express package at work. In it was my manuscript and what I considered then a nice rejection letter. The editor said she didn't think I was quite ready for a book and that it was a bit much to expect people to spend twenty dollars on a book by someone they had never heard of, no matter how good it was. I felt sad, but only for a short while. I continued to send out my synopsis and waited for responses.

A few weeks later I received another letter asking to see my manuscript. This one was from Chronicle Books in San Francisco. Being local, I thought I might actually have an edge. I made color copies of the photos I envisioned in my book, wrote a nice note and hand-delivered my manuscript to their office.

By this time I was frequenting bookstores, looking at what kinds of books were on the market. A book of short stories I noticed turned out to be published by Chronicle Books, so I bought it, thinking it would give me an idea of the kinds of books that they did. Then I read in a free weekly newspaper that the editor who requested my manuscript would be sitting on a panel on publishing sponsored by a Bay Area non-profit organization. I thought it would be a great opportunity to meet him and learn more about the industry, so I scraped up my fifty dollars and headed to San Francisco on a Saturday afternoon.

I found the panel helpful and took notes. It was a great way to start my education on the publishing industry. During the lunch break I made my way to the Chronicle Books editor and introduced myself. I later referred to this meeting in the letter I sent with my manuscript.

In the end, the editor responded by saying that he thought I was a good writer, but didn't think I was "quite right" for Chronicle Books. He also said that my book read like a well-written journal. I remember thinking to myself: and what the hell is wrong with that?

Months after I signed my contract I just missed seeing this same man at the American Bookseller's Convention. I stopped by the Chronicle Books booth and asked for him but they said he had stepped away. I wanted to share my good fortune with him, but with the excitement of the convention forgot to go back to their booth. He had wished me luck in his rejection letter so I thought he might be interested to know that I actually found a publisher.

Rejection

When people ask me how I deal with rejection, I just tell them that I use it as fuel to keep pushing. Once I get over the initial shock and stop my bout of whining, I usually conclude that that was not the right place for me or I wouldn't have been rejected in the first place.

I was completely prepared to be told no over and over again, so I sort of took my rejection letters with a grain of salt. Especially for some of the reasons people were giving me. When I got the letter from Doubleday, I was happy that they even responded at all. But I realized that their advice, to be honest, was full of shit. The editor who responded told me to get published in small literary magazines first, to establish a market for myself. I thought, everyone has to start somewhere! It was a Catch-22 situation: nobody wants to give you the time of day unless you are published, yet nobody wants to publish first-time writers.

This is why it is important to really believe in what you are doing. If I had listened to the Doubleday editor, I would have given up on trying to get my book published and started sending my stuff out to magazines instead (and you would not be reading this book right now).

Sometimes you find you have to practice what you preach. Once I gave an actress friend a lecture on dealing with bad reviews. At the time I had no idea that I would need to follow my own advice one day. She doesn't read reviews because if they are bad she can't take it. I told her that a bad review is only one person's opinion and that their opinion can be influenced by any number of things. They could have had a fight with their spouse before coming to see your show, putting them in a rotten mood, and they ended up picking on you. Or, even if the person genuinely did think you were bad, so what? That is only their opinion -- which of course they are entitled to. I told her, "As long as you do the best job that you possibly can, don't trip off of what other people say about you or your work."

Easier said than done. Several years later I got my first bad book review and was so distraught I almost started crying. Now, my reaction is funny to me. The only thing I need to be concerned with is how my book is selling and if my readers can relate to my work. If that's the case then I do not need to worry about the opinion of someone who could just be mad at me for being young. I later found out that she was married to someone White which made me think maybe my views on interracial relationships were offensive to her.

Success
The third and last positive response I got would be The One. When Glenn Thompson of Writers & Readers called to request my manuscript, I had sent out so

many letters I didn't know who he was or recognize the name of his company.

I remember being surprised by the fact that Writers & Readers was a Black-owned company. During our conversation Glenn told me about a book they had recently published about Black women and self-empowerment called *Tapping the Power Within*, so I went out and bought it. I ended up buying two or three more to give to my friends. I was impressed with the book and even more with the fact that Writers & Readers had published it. That definitely made me feel good about signing with them. It's a good idea to pay attention to who publishes what so you will know the company you will be keeping. You can call publishers to request their current catalog, they come out seasonally.

I sent Glenn my manuscript, but a few weeks later he called to say that he had never received it. Just as I was about to freak out he told me that he was coming to California for a meeting with his distribution company and could get a copy of my manuscript then. Of course I had other copies, but I could not believe that one of the most important things I had ever mailed in my life got lost in the mail! This is a prime example of why it's so important to always have more than one copy of your work: a hard copy and a back-up disk. Glenn came out and we had lunch. The next day he told me he liked what I had written and wanted to publish it, but that he needed to take it back to New York to see what other people in the office thought.

Much later that I wondered, why would the owner of a company have to see what other folks in the office think before taking on a project? Later I found out that that signing new projects is a collaborative effort at Writers & Readers. That made me nervous about whether or not someone in the office would think that doing my book would not be a good idea.

There was no need to worry. Shortly thereafter I got a letter from Deborah Dyson, Writers & Reader's associate publisher, telling me they wanted to publish my book and that with some development they thought it could do extremely well.

I had not expected for the whole thing to happen so quickly, but I was on my way.

Contracts, Advances & Royalties

I will say this right off the bat: it is very difficult to become rich as a writer. People always want to know how and why I still kept my "day job" if I had a book out -- a book that was actually selling. Simple: I still had to pay my rent! If you are trying to get rich quick, you may want to consider another route. Most other published writers I have met have full time jobs to support themselves.

I knew nothing about contracts, so when mine came in the mail from Writers & Readers I immediately found the name of a literary agent from the sister of one of my friends and asked her how much she would charge me to review a contract, to make sure I wasn't getting ripped off. She said $25, so I sent it to her and she said it was standard.

My understanding of how a contract works is that the publisher will offer the writer an advance and a percentage of each book that is sold. An advance is just that: an advance on your book sales. This means that your book must earn that money back before you will receive a percentage from future sales.

Some writers get huge advances which allow them to quit their jobs and write full time. My advance was small, about the same as a month's salary. I received half upon signing the contract and the other half when the book came out. The amount didn't bother me because I was just happy to have my book published. Besides, at that point I had no idea how much books sold for or what writers were getting for their work. This is where having an agent, someone who knows the business, can be in your best interest.

The percentage of the book price that goes to the author is called a royalty. This percentage varies from -- hold on to your seat -- ten to fifteen percent. A first-time author will probably get ten percent. In other words, if your book sells for $21.95, you will get $2.19 (though sometimes that percentage goes up after a certain number of books are sold). When I saw this percentage I was amazed! It seemed to me that the writer, the creator of the work, gets the least of everybody. With that small percentage, you have to sell quite a few books to really make any money. That is, of course, unless you get a huge advance.

When my publisher called to tell me that I had earned my advance back, I was like, "Oh. So how is the weather in New York?" I had no idea what that meant until a week later when I calculated it up. Then I got really excited. I had sold over eight hundred books in a couple of weeks, which was great! It meant that a percentage of the books sold from that point on would be money coming to me in a royalty check. So that was an upside to getting a meager advance: bigger royalty checks.

My publisher does royalty statements twice a year (I had no problem figuring that bit of information out in the contract). My book came out in May of 1995 and in January of 1996 I got my first royalty statement, for the January to June 1995 period. It showed the number of books sold in the previous six months, multiplied by the percentage I get. My advance was deducted, as was a certain amount for returns. In its first two months on the market, my book sold over four thousand copies. My first royalty check was by far the most money I had ever received at one time.

Agents

For some reason it never crossed my mind to get an agent before I tried to get a contract. Probably because although I had heard of agents, I didn't know what they actually did.

An agent is a person who sells manuscripts to publishers on behalf of the writer. Their job is to negotiate with the publisher and get you the best deal possible. For this, they get a percentage of whatever they negotiate (usually somewhere between fifteen and twenty percent).

My first knowledge of how important an agent can be came from reading that April Sinclair, author of *Coffee Will Make You Black*, got a six-figure advance for a two-book deal which were her first published writings. Needless to say, she quit her full time job to write. Another Bay Area writer I met told me she got a six-figure advance for her first book as well. Both of these women had agents. Really good ones, apparently.

Even though I landed my first contract without the help of an agent, I probably would have gotten a much better deal financially had I had someone who knew the business acting on my behalf. Now, as I continue my career as a writer, I feel it is imperative to have an agent. I don't mind giving someone fifteen percent of whatever they get me, since I know it is probably more than I would get on my own. In this sense, a good agent may even pay for themselves.

The thing about getting an agent is that they have to really connect with your work. Many times they turn first-time authors down. It's hard trying to convince someone to take a chance on a new author. Evelyn White gave me the name of her agent, one of the most well-known Black female agents in New York. It took me months to muster up the courage to send her a letter and when I did, she sent a letter back saying that she was not accepting new clients. My feelings were hurt but I got over it. I was happy to get a letter at all; another friend got her query back from the same agent with a rejection note scrawled across the front of it!

Another writer I know told me about an independent agent in Palo Alto. She came highly recommended by this writer, who had been writing longer than me and had several experiences with agents. I sent the agent a letter asking her to call if she would like a press packet and a book. She did, we spoke, and I got a clear sense of what she was about from our brief conversation. She told me it wouldn't do either of us any good for her to say she would represent me at that point. She didn't want to hear about my "great ideas", she wanted to see what I had actually done. Since my first book was sold, she said, there was nothing to do but start working on selling the next one. Generally, you need more than a paragraph on what a book is about to do that. She said she would need to see a chapter-by-chapter outline of my next book, along with two sample chapters. This is where having your book proposal or manuscript ready and waiting would be to your advantage. I appreciated her honesty and it inspired me to get my butt in gear.

The type of agent and relationship you have with them is really up to personal preference. Some writers are not interested in having a relationship with their agent whatsoever; all they want is for their work to be sold. Some folks could care less if it's a Black person, a woman, or whatever. For me, these are important things to consider. I want someone who will be genuinely interested in the quality of my work and who will work wholeheartedly to get me the best deal possible. In other words, I really want to connect with the person who will be getting fifteen percent of my earnings.

Oddly enough, finding an agent has been harder for me than finding a publisher was. I am still without one! I did not expect to have such a hard time finding someone to represent me. I say over and over that I would much rather have someone tell me no than to sign a contract with them and have them put my stuff in a slush pile and not try to sell it. I always thought that the hardest part would be selling the first book, and if it did OK, getting an agent for next one would be smooth sailing. For now I just continue to work on my projects so that when I find the right person I will have material for them. It will be nice to focus less on finding an agent or publisher and more on my writing.

I do not recommend acting as your own agent unless you have a legal background, can negotiate and have a vast knowledge of the publishing industry. The average person has no idea what their own work is worth, nor do they have the contacts in the publishing industry that an agent will. A good agent can read about a project and know immediately which editor at which house to call to solicit the book. Some publishing houses won't even deal with writers, only their agents.

Hardback vs. Paperback

When I heard that my book was going to cost $17.95 I nearly had a fit. I remember thinking, "Damn, I rarely pay that much for a book." I wanted the book to cost $10. Ah, ignorance. Glenn Thompson told me that $17.95 was cheap for a hardback book. I went to the bookstore to price other hardbacks, and of course, he was right. Not only that, at my first book signing I sold forty-four books in two hours. That made me realize that price might not really be an issue. I also didn't understand at first that eventually the book would come out in paperback and that the paperback would cost $10.

Hardback books have a longer shelf life, and, from what I am told, carry more credibility. Often when a book comes out in hardback it is followed by a paperback edition, and my publisher told me that when the paperback comes out it is almost like a new book; they send out press information all over again. This gives a book a longer shelf life as well. Usually hardback books come out in paperback a year or so after the initial release. Sometimes there are two versions, a trade paperback and a mass paperback. The trade is larger, usually 5"X7" and the mass paperback is the smaller version you see near supermarket checkout stands.

The Book Itself

Just like I had no say in whether or not my book would be hardback or soft, I had no say in a lot of other things about it. My contract stated that the publisher would have the last word on different aspects such as the design, cover, title, etc. This is very common. I guess the rationale is that a publisher knows more about what is appealing to the public than a writer does.

My friend Monique Gilmore caught hell from everyone over the cover of her first book. You'll remember that Monique is a romance novelist. Her first book had a light-skinned, half white-looking woman on the cover looking dreamily into the camera, blue eyes and all. This would have been fine and good had her main character, Georgette, not been described as the complete opposite!

Unless you plan to self-publish, do not get too attached to your title or cover idea. Both may end up being totally different than what you had in mind. My book was originally titled *Nappy Edges*. But around the time it was supposed to come out, Ntozake Shange's novel *Lilliane* was published, along with a lot of her other work, including a book of poems called --guess what -- *Nappy Edges*. Of course we discovered this after my book had been listed in thousands of Fall catalogs for the distribution company and circulated at sales conferences. Which is why, to this day, in every bookstore computer system my book is listed as *Nappy Edges*.

Eventually, my publisher decided on just *Nappy* and a subtitle. I hated it. I wrote them a letter expressing my feelings. I felt that the word "nappy" was an adjective and didn't sit well by itself, so I sent them a list of other suggestions: "Nappy-Headed," "Nappy Kitchen, "Nappy Roots," "Nappy & Happy," etc. Just plain "nappy" started growing on me when I saw Malik Yoba on the television show "New York Undercover" with a sweatshirt that said "NAPPY" on it in big, bold letters. It also happens to be the name of a clothing line popular in the hiphop community. Who knew? Seeing this helped me to make peace with the title.

Initially, I also had a problem with the cover of my book. I had given Glenn a bunch of pictures I envisioned could be used with it, and a few months after signing the contract, I received a color copy of the cover in the mail, which used one of the photos I had submitted. Immediately I called Writers & Readers and expressed my concern again. I didn't know exactly what I wanted on the cover, but I knew it wasn't my face! A lot of books I had noticed lately had artwork in them, like those by Varnette Honeywood and Cynthia St. James. I thought something like that would be nice. Then someone reminded me that it was not free to use an artist's work on the cover of a book. That was something I had not thought of.

Deborah Dyson had a long conversation with me about the cover, telling me how wonderful it was and how as a new author I needed something striking. She explained that sometimes a cover can sell a book, and being that I was new on the scene, that would benefit me. I liked Deborah and knew she wouldn't just tell me any old thing. My best friend's aunt said the same thing and proved to be instrumental in helping me to not give my publisher a hard time about it.

Well, needless to say, I get tons of compliments on the cover of my book. People love it. My high school friend Seti was on her way to the restroom at Cody's Books in Berkeley and stopped in her tracks when she saw my face on the cover. She didn't know I had written a book and was totally surprised. She recognized instantly that it was me and absolutely loved the cover. And once when I went to the copy store to get enlargements made, the young woman working there asked me if she could make a copy of my book cover for herself.

The graphic designer who did the layout for my book did a wonderful job. As my friend Boo says, "she hooked it up." Well before I even thought about doing a book I read *Once Upon a Time When We Were Colored* by Clifton Taulbert. Since I love photographs, I was particularly struck by the way his book looked; each chapter started with a collage of photos, and I thought it was gorgeous. This is why I gave photos to Glenn Thompson along with my manuscript. Writers & Readers ended up using them with great care to construct a beautiful-looking book. I consider myself lucky, since the author usually has so little to do with this aspect of the publishing process.

The Finished Product

When I finally saw my book for the first time I was at work. I received yet another express mail package, but this time it was the first two finished copies of my book I'd ever seen. I was excited and shared the book with my co-workers who had been hearing about it from the very beginning.

I wasn't totally shocked bcause I had seen a galley (the graphically designed version unbound and without a cover) a few weeks before. It was then that the cover didn't seem so bad after all. I noticed they put my picture on the back cover, which meant I was on the front and the back!

The fact that I had a book out didn't really sink in until I started seeing and hearing about it in public. I got really excited when I walked into Marcus Bookstore one day and saw a man I didn't know buying *Nappy*. Shanna, a young woman who works there and always reads my work, told him I was the author and had me sign it. Then a couple of people told me they saw folks on public transportation reading *Nappy*, too. I was waiting for that to happen so I could tap the person and tell them they were reading my book!

One of the best experiences happened at a book expo. I had stepped away from the Writers & Readers booth and when I came back, a young woman in her early twenties had my book in her hand and was telling her friend, "Girl, this book is the bomb. I loved it. You need to read it." Naturally I told her it was mine and and was so happy to hear that she liked it. When she realized I was the author we hugged like we knew each other. To my surprise, I ended up being on the receiving end of lots of hugs.

The Publishing Industry

I can't say it enough, the more you know, the better off
you are. The publishing industry is no different from
any other industry. If you don't know what's up you can
end up in a situation that is not in your best interest.
Take it upon yourself to learn as much about the industry as you can. A bookstore owner told me once that
she thought writers get treated really bad in the industry. It might be because people think we are stupid for
not knowing the business side of being an author.

American Booksellers Association

Going to the annual American Booksellers Convention
can give you a real sense of the publishing industry. I
went for the first time in May of 1994, when the convention was held in Los Angeles. I had just signed
with my publisher, and even though my book wasn't
in stores yet, I decided to go. (The publishing industry
was still so new to me I was up for any opporunity to
learn more about it.) Plus, Deborah and Beth from
my publisher's office were going to be there and I
thought it would be a good opportunity to meet them.

The only book-related convention I had been to pre-
viously was the San Francisco Book Festival, a week-
end expo for book lovers held each November. The
ABA convention is different because it is a trade
show-an opportunity for people in the publishing
industry to network and display their new projects.
All kinds of publishers are present to hand out information on their companies and products. Authors
are there to promote their books, and there are lots of

receptions and parties going on.

What I remember most about the convention was how huge it was. It seemed like miles and miles of convention space filled to capacity with books and publishers on everything you could possibly think of. Promotional posters, bookmarks, flyers, bags and buttons were being handed out everywhere. I collected several catalogs from different companies I remembered seeing in The Literary Marketplace, the huge book I used to find all of the publishers in the country.

I wasn't expecting it, so when I approached the Writers & Readers booth and saw my face on an enlarged book cover I got both nervous and excited. It was definitely an eye catcher! It was a trip to sit at the booth and watch people respond to the cover. Even though no one seemed to suspect it was me, I think that was the first time I actually realized I was about to be an author.

Of course, I did notice the scarcity of Black publishers at the ABA convention. The community that were there kind of huddled together and everyone seemed to know each other. I went to a reception sponsored by the Blackboard List, an organization that does a bestseller list of books by Black authors (you can find this in *Essence* magazine or the *Quarterly Black Review of Books*) and was so intimidated I basically sat there eating and checking out the scene. Had it been a year later, when I'd gotten over my shyness at promoting my work, I wouldn't have missed this great opportunity to network and pass out flyers.

The ABA convention happens every year in Chicago. It's a great chance to meet and greet people in the publishing industry up close and personal. If you ever get a chance to go, do it! Book festivals are smaller versions of ABA, I highly recommend going to as many book festivals as you can. There are lots of valuable resources and good places to meet people in the industry such as agents and editors. Go and practice networking!

Specialized Publishers

Random House, Doubleday and Viking are not the only way to get your book published. There are over 300 publishers in the country and only about a dozen of these are the major houses. Starting off with one of the other 288 is probably a more realistic goal. Small and independent publishing houses are far more likely to take a chance on first-time authors. Small and independent houses are usually more inclined to take a risk on a new writer but the cash flow is not always in the best interest of the author. In other words, you may or may not get paid when you are supposed to or get your book promoted the way it should.

Just as there are Black-owned and female-owned publishing companies, there are companies that specialize in other specific types of books. After taking a trip around the world, my friend Elaine Lee decided to put together an anthology of Black women's travel stories. *Go Girl: The Black Woman's Book of Travel and Adventure* was accepted and published by a small press that does travel books by and for women. How perfect is that?

This is why being familiar with who publishes what is important. If you do your research, chances are you'll find a company that specializes in the type of book you are planning to do.

Black Publishers

Deep down, I feel that had it not been for Writers & Readers, *Nappy* probably never would have been published. Most people in business are not into taking risks because you have to be prepared to lose money if you invest in a project that doesn't do well. In my case they thought it was a project that had potential, and luckily, they had a vision for it.

Books are documentation of our history and experiences. So it makes sense that what we think is worthy of becoming a book might (and usually does) differ from what more mainstream houses might feel is important enough to be published. Some of the books currently on the market might have never been published or remained in print had it not been for Black publishers. Would *A Hundred Years of Lynchings*, a book that lists by state all of the reported lynchings in the country over a hundred year period, have been re-published if it were not for Black Classic Press in Baltimore? I don't think so. It's an important book. Painful, but important.

Sometimes people lose all sense of themselves and

their convictions when it comes to money. I have heard that many writers wouldn't dream of doing a book with a Black publisher if they can take their work to a more mainstream company and get ten times more money. Well, I want to get paid too, but I can't imagine that I would ever not support my own people. It gives me great pride to tell people that my book was published by a Black-owned company.

Black-owned publishing houses, like any other type of Black-owned business, need the support of our community. Just like buying from Black-owned stores helps them stay in business, writers need to do business with Black publishers so that they, too, will stay in business.

Doin' it Yourself

If you are up for more than just writing and promoting your work, self publishing might be for you. The whole process is described in great detail in a book called *The Self Publishing Manual*, which I list in the reference section of this book. When you self publish your book you cut out the middle person, instead of getting ten or fifteen percent of each book sold, you get all of the money. Except for wholesale to bookstores in which you get about sixty percent, depending on your agreement with the store.

There are printing companies which not only make your books but for small fees will handle a lot of the logistics involved in publishing your own book such as graphic design and layout, getting a copyright,

ISBN # and getting a bar code.

Vanity Presses (Subsidy Press)
In the back of most magazines there is a classified section. Usually there is an ad there for getting your
book published, near the "get the long beautiful hair
you've always wanted" ads, which makes me a little
suspicious. Most of the time, these are ads for vanity
presses. A vanity press is a publishing company you
pay to publish your book. They claim that for one fee
they will produce your "quality" book, promote it and
distribute it. I don't know how much they charge or
how good the quality is, but I am leery of anyone who
charges a fee just to read your work.

Not only that, by the time you pay someone else to do
your book, you could have taken a fraction of the
money and published it yourself! The one person I
know who used a vanity press is a woman named
Carol Denise Simms. She wrote a very moving and
emotional book called *What Happened to Suzy*, and
her company ended up going out of business. Most
people use vanity presses because they are unaware of
their options which is why it's so important to know
as much as you can about the industry and what
you're getting into. Do your homework!

Self-Publishing
Self publishing was never an option for me. I never
even considered it, because although I was working,
when I started writing my book I was flat broke, so the
idea of coming up with enough money to make a

book was out of the question. To self publish you have to have a little bit of money stashed away. Actually more than a little money, because once you get the books done you need money to distribute them to various stores (which, if you want to go national, can be costly). Then it takes money to promote your book, or you run the risk of ending up with several hundred copies which you may have to give out as Christmas presents to everyone you know!

If I had been turned down by enough publishers, self-publishing would have eventually entered my mind. I read that E. Lynn Harris self published his book *Invisible Life* at first, before Doubleday picked it up. He spent his entire life savings to do it. This was the first I heard of someone self-publishing a novel.

My favorite self-publishing story is that of Lonnice Brittnum Bonner, who wrote a book called *Good Hair: For Colored Girls Who've Considered A Weave When The Chemicals Became Too Rough.* I read an article about her in the Oakland Tribune (she was living in Oakland at the time) and rushed out to buy her book. I couldn't believe that her 100-page book cost $16.95, but then I found out that she self-published it and made a limited amount. She had to charge that much just to break even, probably. Well, the book sold completely out of the run she made and was picked up by Crown Trade paperback which then put the book on the market for $10.00. I don't know for sure, but it would not surprise me to learn that she could not get her book published by a publisher at

first. It's very common for a large house to be interested in a book that was self published after they see
that there is an interest in it and it has done well.

Self Publishing Interviews
I have a few friends who did self publish their own
books. In this section they will share the advantages
and disadvantages of self publishing.

First is Nancy E. Johnson, a wonderful performance
poet I met in April, 1995 when I did an event with four
other Black women writers called "Our Black Bodies." I
was really moved by her work and invited her to do a
couple of readings with me. Her work (now a book of
poems) is called *Sex, Love & Reproduction*. Alvis O.
Davis writes relationship books. I met him at the
Today's Black Woman Expo in Chicago. He was very
nice and besides passing my name along to people in
the media, he gave me names of bookstores and publications that might be of use. He seemed to really be
going at it full force and his books have done well.
Finally, poet Jeff Jones had what I consider the ultimate
chapbook experience. A chapbook is an inexpensive
booklet of the poets work. To date he has sold close to
3,000 copies of his first, self-published chapbook.

Nancy Elizabeth Johnson
Nancy Johnson noticed an interest in her work
appearing in book form through the various events
she did. People often asked her if a book of her
poems was available. (After hearing her read and seeing her perform it was easy to see why.)

Nancy says that aside from the fact that she didn't feel like waiting for her "lucky moment" from a publisher, her decision to self publish stemmed from her tendency to be independent. She did what most independent spirits would: took matters into her own hands!

The biggest obstacle Nancy faced in self publishing was coming up with the money to do it. That and finding someone to design and print her book. Luckily, Nancy had the good fortune of being able to count on her family in time of need; various family members pulled together and gave (not loaned) her the money to produce her first book. Finding someone with experience to help guide her was not as easy. Nancy ended up using a graphic artist referred to her by someone she knew and calling around for estimates of what the final product would cost.

Although she was pretty satisfied with the way it came out, Nancy says that if she had to do it all over again she would try to get more involved in the process, possibly taking a desktop publishing course to become more familiar with layout and design. She would also make sure she had a signed written agreement with the printer before commissioning them to do the work, so they can't tell you one thing in the beginning and do something entirely different in the end (her book is staple-bound instead of perfect bound, which is what she requested initially.)

As for distribution and promotion, Nancy admits to

not having enough time to work on these aspects of self publishing. A month after the book's completion, it was available in only one Bay Area bookstore (proudly displayed in the front window), where she did a reading with two other local writers.

Nancy has sent out a promotional postcard of the book cover announcing the book's arrival on the scene. She sent it to all the names and addresses she has been collecting over the months since first deciding to publish her work. She continues to collect names and addresses at all of her performances. Eventually Nancy would like her work to be available on a national level, particularly at bookstores and theaters where she performs.

Alvis Davis
Alvis Davis' first self-published book, *The Cold Reality: How to Get and Keep a Black Man in a Relationship*, has sold over twenty thousand copies since its release in 1990. That's a lot of books, considering the fact that his first print run was only two thousand.

Alvis chose to self publish because he thought that the nature of his book would not appeal to most mainstream publishers. Also, when he saw the percentage writers earn from each book sale, he decided to publish the book on his own.

Alvis decided to use money put away he had been planning to use for a car to self publish his nonfiction book on relationships. Deciding to do it was the easy part. The hard part was educating himself on every single aspect of the process. His greatest challenge was having to oversee every detail from the first sentence to the completed book.

Alvis strongly suggests doing your homework before investing time and money in self publishing, and if nothing else, hiring an editor. He feels mistakes made on his first book could have been avoided had he taken the time to do his homework rather than blindly taking on the task. He does admit to being smart enough to go to the library for information throughout the process.

Alvis went to the Yellow Pages to find a printer for his first print run. He paid almost $4000. After researching other printers in the country at the library, he found a printer to do his books for half that price (again, DO YOUR HOMEWORK!) Alvis warns that using an out-of-state printer will cost more for shipping, but that you might save money in the long run. In most cases you will have to pay half when placing your order and the other half when the books are done.

Alvis says his most valuable lesson was the difference between advertising and publicity (explained in Section 3). He took out an ad in *Essence* magazine for around two thousand dollars. "The ad paid for itself," he remembers, "but now I wouldn't pay for advertising or suggest that others do it." This is because later, during the promotion process, Alvis learned that you can get a great deal of publicity for free.

A friend hooked him up with BET (Black Entertainment Television), where he did a nationally syndicated show with Bev Smith. That set things off- and it didn't cost him a cent! Book orders soared after that kind of exposure. From that experience he was able to tap into Black radio shows around the country.

Alvis continues to handle all of his own distribution and promotion. He says that of 350 Black-owned bookstores nationwide, his books are in most of them. From visiting the library, he found out the names and addresses of the major black distribution companies.

One important thing Alvis recommends for people who choose to self publish is to get their book listed in the annual publication "Books in Print." He says this is an absolute must! You can find this book in the reference section of any public library and most bookstores. Being listed there will enable stores who don't carry your book to get in contact with you to place an order.

"Self publishing is a lot of work, but it can definitely pay off." Alvis says. With two books out, he has sold approximately 30,000 books since first deciding to self publish. His second book, *Black Men Not Looking For Sex*, is in its second printing. His last words of advice to those wishing to self publish their work is, once again, to DO YOUR HOMEWORK to avoid costly mistakes and self publish only if you are committed to what you write, because it can be a lot of work. It can also be very rewarding.

Jeff Jones
Jeff Jones, a young gay Black man, has had his poetry published in in several anthologies and magazines. It wasn't until a few years ago when he decided to self-publish a chapbook that he got a full-fledged lesson on the publishing industry -- a lesson that spanned three years.

He got the idea while recuperating from having his tonsils taken out. After writing about two hundred poems he spent several months editing and deciding which ones to use for his book. He began by typing in and printing out all the poems, then he put them in the order he wanted them to appear in the chapbook.

Jeff had an idea of how he wanted the cover to look from the very beginning, so he hired an artist to create it. It turned out so well his friends started making t-shirts and sweatshirts with the design on them. One of his friends even had it silk-screened on a bed spread as a gift.

He called around before settling for the first estimate he got from a printer, and found a big difference in the prices each printer quoted him. He was not impressed with any of the quotes he'd been given and decided to continue to look around. One day he just walked into a printing company near his home and asked for an estimate. They gave him a great price, and the rest is history! Initially he had four hundred copies of his chapbook printed and it cost him five hundred and fifty dollars. This price reflected the printing cost alone since he gave them camera-ready artwork for the cover and the text was graphically designed in the layout he wanted for the book. The only thing the printer had to do was print the books. NOTE: Once again, this is a prime example of how knowing how to use a desktop publishing program can help and save you money.

As soon as the books were ready, Jeff sent fifty copies to his mother to keep for the family archives. Smart move -- the other three hundred and fifty sold in two days! He eventually raised his price from five to eight dollars, which, after seeing the book, I still thought was a steal! He actually made enough money from sales to pay for promotional trips to New York, Washington D.C., Chicago, Atlanta and Los Angeles.

Jeff's book did so well because he had a very support-ive family and group of friends who helped get the word out. At his first reading some of his friends bought ten and twenty copies of the book to give to other people as presents. He also honed in on a very specific audience and sought out every possible angle and opportunity to promote his book. He organized readings and also read at gay conferences and writing seminars. His book was reviewed in national gay publi-cations, which is unheard of for mainstream publications.

As a publicity plan, he sent a press release and order

form to all the gay bookstores in the country and even some abroad. He also had postcards of the book cover printed to give out. Contacting the bookstores resulted in having several stores carry his book. This arrangement is a sixty-forty split, which means of the sales the author gets sixty and the store forty percent. He attributes about one third of his total sales to bookstores. Most of them he peddled himself.

Jeff told me that the most rewarding part of his experience was going from a mere idea to the actual finished product. The response he got was also quite rewarding. He warns that self-publishing a chapbook is a lot of work but may be the best way to get your work out there. It is the only way you will be able to do your book the exact way you want it to be done. And I think there is definitely something to be said for that.

For Black Writers...

Section 3: Promoting Your Book

Once your book is published, a whole new job begins: getting the word out about it. After all, what good is it to have a book out if nobody knows it's there?

Publicity should not be confused with advertising. Advertising is when you pay to promote your product; publicity is free. Buying an ad on the radio or in a newspaper is advertising. Doing an interview or being the subject of an article is publicity, free of charge.

Still, it's more than a notion to get a story on you or your book in a newspaper or magazine. Most publishers have publicists or a publicity department who are responsible for generating interest in their product; often when you see a book featured it means a publicist approached the publication about doing it. I learned most of what I know about this process during the year I worked for Ave Montague, an independent San Francisco publicist who handles arts-related events.

Though I knew Writers & Readers would do something for Nappy, since it was my first book I figured I might need some extra help. I couldn't afford to pay a professional publicist, so I decided to use what I already knew and become my own.

My Peace of Mind Campaign

Around that time I also read an article by Terry McMillan in the *Quarterly Black Review of Books* which described what she did to promote her first book, *Mama*. McMillan explained that she sent out 4,000 letters all over the country telling people about her book, mailing them to national organizations, newspapers and magazines, radio and TV stations, Black colleges and Black and women's studies' departments. I photocopied this article and vowed to follow exactly what she did, step by step and then some!

I decided to do my own letters and flyers. In what I called my "letter of support" I asked people to post my flyer, pass it on to someone else who might find it interesting, or, if they were really moved by it, to make copies and give them out. At the end I thanked them for their support.

Producing the flyers was one of those many instances where it would have helped me to know a graphics computer program. I wanted to give my business to a Black woman, but she quoted me $150.00 for a simple design and I just couldn't afford it. So, a co-worker who was also a graphic artist did a simple flyer for me in exchange for lunch. I had five thousand flyers printed on brightly colored paper and by the time I finished my Peace of Mind publicity campaign, as I called it, I had only a small stack of a hundred or so left.

For my first five events I also had a postcard made. To be cost effective I had the same design printed four times on one page and photocopied this onto heavy paper. I made 400 made and sent them out to everyone on my personal mailing list.

Letters

All of the flyers I mailed out were accompanied by a letter, either my "letter of support" or one written for the specific situation. For instance, I did a letter especially for Black-owned businesses in the Bay Area highlighting the fact that I was a local author, and a more sisterly letter for people from a mailing list of Black women's support groups that I got in the mail.

Each and every opportunity I saw to get the word out about my book, I took. Thumbing through *Ebony* magazine I saw a story on Black women college presidents that listed the schools where each of them presided, so I sent each a flyer and a special, personalized letter as well. A few of them even took the time to write back and thank me, assuring me they would post the flyer to help my efforts.

When my book finally came out I wrote a letter to all of the bookstores in the Bay Area telling them I was local and available for readings and signings. I wanted them to know that I lived in Oakland and was prepared to do anything within my power to promote my book. This may be one reason why nine months after it came out, the poster of my book cover was still in the window of local bookstores. It felt good to have that kind of support, and it really helped my sales, I'm sure.

Promotional Materials

My Peace of Mind campaign was in addition to traditional promotional duties which include sending out a variety of material to the media. Following are a few items essential to promoting a book:

Press Releases - Press releases are the first and foremost tool of self-promotion. They come in handy and you will need lots of them.

A press release is a basic who, what, when, where and why fact sheet about you and your book. They usually start with a heading. My first one read: "Local Author Promotes First Book in Bay Area." I sent about 40 copies of it out to the local print media (both the weekly and daily papers), the public affairs departments of all of the radio stations, the producers of television talk shows, local magazine editors and anyone else whose name I had seen who I thought might be interested in giving my book some exposure.

Press Packets - A press packet is for people who need more than just a little information. The elements of a press packet can vary. Mine had fourteen clips and reviews from different publications topped with a press release, as well as an author resume, black and white head shot and color brochure from my publisher. I placed these items in a clean, two-pocket folder, tucked a business card into the space provided and added an 11"x17" color copy of the cover of the book which I folded in half to fit in the folder. If I had gotten one I would have pasted a copy of my cover to the front of the folder. I ended up making color copies of the cover to glue on the front of the folder.

It's not necessary to send this much stuff to everyone.

It can be very costly and if you are not sure that they will need it, there's always the chance that it could get thrown away. However, the elements of a good press packet usually include:

Author resume - An author resume differs from a standard resume in that it lists exclusively your accomplishments as an author. It should give an idea of what you have done to promote your book. Mine listed all of the places I had done book-related events, by date, divided into categories: Bookstores, Schools, Panels, Expos and Conferences. Bookstores went first because I had done the most events in those.

Clippings - In addition to being good for exposure, reviews can also serve as material to encourage others to help you. They increase your credibility. "Clips" are photocopies of these reviews from newspapers and magazines. You should always make sure that the publication and date are included on the copy. I had a few favorite articles which I kept on hand and whenever I sent anybody something regarding my book, I sent copies of the articles. Having extra copies on hand is nice because I sent them out as much as I sent my publicity flyer out, which was often.

Flyer - I had a flyer announcing the publication of the book and they were very helpful in promoting my book. I had them printed in neon colors and sent them out to any and everyone. It had the cover of the book, a few sentences on what the book was about, a short bio on me and a few words about my publisher.

I also included the publication date which was dated once the book went into a second printing. It didn't matter, I just hand-wrote on the flyer that the book had gone into a second printing. Flyers are less expensive then postcards so I recommend having a flyer made if you can't afford postcards. Also, if you self publish your book, you can make the bottom part of the flyer an order form.

Head Shots - Working with Ave Montague taught me how important publicity photos can be. Visual aids are always good, and besides, if someone decides to do a story right away you won't have to worry about hooking up a photo because they'll already have one. An interesting photo may even attract someone's attention enough to encourage them to read your material.

Unfortunately, I absolutely hate having my picture taken! When my publisher told me they needed a current head shot I almost said, "Can't you just crop one of those pictures I already sent you?" The pictures I sent were old and rather dated, so that was not an option.

Jim Dennis, the photographer I hired to take my picture, was quite helpful in dealing with my discomfort. Besides being a great photographer I liked him very much as a person, so our session went really well. He sent me a contact sheet with twelve poses on it and I pondered them for a few days, getting input from my friends. I ended up very happy with my choice.

Apparently my publisher was too, since they put the photo on the back cover of my book.

I knew from the jump that I wanted a head shot that looked as much like me as possible -- the real me. A very natural-looking picture, so that nobody would mistake me for somebody else. Jim helped me to feel really comfortable and I was careful not to overdress or put on too much makeup, so my photo turned out exactly how I wanted it to.

In the beginning I had ten copies of my head shot made each time I needed them. It was expensive, but I could never afford to have a larger quantity made. Then I found a company that does head shots for the-atrical models and actors. They produced my photo in a large quantity and at a great price -- 500 copies cost less than having 100 custom-printed. The photos were printed on cardstock instead of regular photo-graphic paper, but they look just as nice and are easi-er to write on. My name, the title of my book and the publisher were printed on the bottom.

Immediately I sent a stack to my publisher, a stack to Ave (who so graciously agreed to help me), and a stack to my parents. With that many photos at my disposal, I was able to give them to bookstores where I would be reading and to anyone else who wanted one. Some bookstores used my photo in newspaper ads to announce their upcoming readings and some used them along with the cover of the book for in-store signs.

I got in the habit of carrying a stack of head shots around in a file folder (you never know when an opportunity to use them might come up!) Once I was at Roscoe's Chicken & Waffles Restaurant in Los Angeles, a restaurant whose walls are covered with head shots and promotional photographs of models and actors, some well-known and some not. I asked a waitress if I could leave one of my photos for them to put up. She politely told me that she would ask the manager. Well, a few months later I ran across a friend who told me he was in Roscoe's in L.A. and saw my picture on the wall. I was very happy that I had taken the time to ask and sent them a card thanking them for their support.

Business Cards and Stationery

Business cards are a very important promotional item. People ask me all the time if they can have my card. They, too, give you credibility.

James Warren gave me his business card once. It blew me away. There was a color reproduction of his book, *The Freeman Field Mutiny*, on it. What a novel idea, I thought. Why didn't I think of that?

I needed something simple and cheap, so I went to a large office supply chain and had 1,000 cards made for $10. My cards didn't have a logo, just my name, the title "writer" underneath and the address of my post office box. I left my phone number off because I didn't want any and everybody calling me at home. Whenever I wanted people to have my number I just wrote it on the back.

One thing I wish I had invested in is personalized stationery. Aside from my form letters, which were photocopied, I sent out quite a few letters that would have been better presented that way. Since there was a laser printer where I worked, I did my own makeshift stationery on computer. I typed "From The Desk Of" with my name and address at the top, centered and in bold type. Maybe not the most creative job, but it worked.

Matching envelopes would have been good, too. I spent hours rubber-stamping the envelopes I sent out for my Peace of Mind campaign. Eventually I graduated to custom-made return address labels ordered from a check printing company. I chose labels with a square of kente cloth pattern in the left hand corner, which looked really nice-so much better than my rubber stamp! How cost effective labels are versus a rubber stamp depends on how many letters you'll be sending out. For 4,000 to 5,000 a rubber stamp may make more sense. On the other hand, sometimes it's worth spending a little extra if you can afford it and the result will make you feel even better about your presentation.

Mailing Lists
In addition to the mailing lists I put together per Terry McMillan's suggestion, a year before my book came out I began collecting the names and addresses of everyone I ran into. I put them in a file folder and periodically added them to one of my many, many

databases. My file folder contained business cards, napkins, matchbook covers -- a whole slew of pieces of paper I had collected over the year. When the time came to send out the first postcard listing my events, I sent one to each person on my list of about 200 names.

A couple of years before I had worked as a tutor to the child actors in a Broadway play in New York. We were given an address list for the cast and crew and for some reason I held on to mine. I was so happy I did; that was over 40 more people all over the country wo whom I could send a letter and a flyer.

Once I decided I was on a mission to get the word out, things just started coming my way. One day I got a lavender-colored booklet in the mail called "A Circle of Sisters Directory." The return address was a large record company in New York. I knew absolutely no one there but was ever so grateful to get the directory. It was a listing of Black women's support groups all over the country and a list of networking sisters. I plugged all this information into my computer too -- about three hundred names.

I even had a file folder for the cities I planned to visit with the names and addresses of people to call on when the time came. The first places I planned to visit were Washington, D.C. and New York, so I put the name and address of the person who reviewed my book for the Washington City Paper in that file along with my New York contacts. I also sent away for information on the 4th Annual National Black Writers

Conference in New York. When I got it, I put the director's name and address in my file so I could invite her to my New York readings.

Not only are mailing lists important for promotion, they can also be a way to make extra money. People will always need mailing lists, but nobody wants to put them together so they will pay for them. Friends of mine who are authors have bought copies of my mailing lists (already on labels) rather than duplicate the work I have done. When my friend Elaine needed to send out a call for submissions for her anthology on Black women travellers, my mailing list of Black women's support groups was exactly what she needed.

Database Programs

The duty I hated most when I started my job as an administrative assistant was creating mailing labels on computer. My experience with database programs was limited, and formatting a label template takes practice. I messed up a whole bunch of labels before I was able to make the layout come out perfectly.

The day I started entering my first mailing list into my computer at home I was so grateful for having had to perfect the task at work. Right away I realized the importance of being able to use this kind of program. It would have been impossible for me to hand-address each envelope I sent out. Signing each letter, stamping my return address and "address correction requested" on each envelope, folding, stuffing and sealing was enough to keep me plenty busy!

I suggest learning -- and mastering -- any database program. They can be costly; I was fortunate to be able to use a program at work and the used computer I bought came loaded with the same one. But if you can get access to one, do it! Being able to print out hundreds of labels at the click of a button will save you more time than you can possibly imagine.

Mass Mailings

I sent letters and flyers to over 3,000 places nation-wide. Financially the postage was overwhelming, which is why some of my letters were late-real late-going out. I researched bulk mail but didn't feel like going through the whole process, which involved paying to get a permit. Plus, when I found out that it would take four weeks to get a letter from California to New York, I decided to "bite the bullet" and buy the stamps.

Months before the book was published I hand-signed, stuffed and sealed letters to everyone on my lists from the McMillan article, and a month before it came out in bookstores I dropped 1,500 pieces of mail in the box. The other 1,500 sat in my living room until I could get the money to buy postage. I did a few hundred at a time until I got them all out. Every bit of money I spent became "how many stamps could that have been?" Depending on how you look at it, my letters were either late for the first printing of my book or just in time for the second!

One thing to anticipate about mass mailings is that people do move and you will get a lot of returns.

Don't freak out. I got letters returned with a new address (be sure to stamp "address correction requested" on everything you mail out) as well as a bunch for which the forwarding order had expired. I kept all of these and later went through and changed or deleted addresses as necessary.

Keeping your mailing lists "clean" will save you time and money. The next time you use a list, or if you decide to sell it, you won't waste your postage or others' sending information to the wrong place.

Target Audience

The best publicity plan involves knowing your primary target audience is and how to reach it. For example, to promote this book I will send a letter and flyer to all of the writing workshops, seminars, and retreats I can find the addresses to. I also found a copy of a magazine which listed over a hundred writing conferences nationwide, they will get a letter and flyer from me as well. So will the forty-one writing organizations and the ninety writing programs at colleges and universities.

You need to be creative in thinking of ways to promote your book. In attending many readings of other authors, I have noticed how often they too get asked how they got their books published. I decided to send a flyer and letter to other authors asking for support. I would like them to be able to recommend this book whenever they get people wanting to know "how to do it." I figured a hundred and fifty is a good round number to start with. The thing about coming up with all of these great ideas of places to mail to is having to enter them into the computer. Once it's in though you can easily use it again when you need to or sell it to someone else who might be able to use it.

Following Up

People in the media get so much stuff from so many people that a friendly phone call might be a good reminder and could help get your materials noticed. Sometimes they might be interested in what you've sent but had no chance to call you so a follow up call can make it more convenient for them. Your making the first move can result in getting what you want.

It's important to do follow-up calls, but because of my full time job, I didn't have much time to do that. Thanks to good receptionists (and now voicemail), a follow-up call doesn't mean you will ever get to the speak to the person you have sent material to.

Local Publications

When I started sending stuff to local newspapers I knew that nobody knew who I was, but figured if I kept at it they would get tired enough of hearing from me to eventually respond. You never know. I went from being annoyed that my events were not listed to being sick of seeing my name in the paper. Once I saw my name in the San Francisco Chronicle's listings four times in the same week!

When media folks get used to getting stuff from you it sometimes encourages special treatment. One popular weekly paper did a full page listing of events for Black History month. I sent them a calendar of nine events and a couple of days later they put some of them in their special listing. I am sure my previous mailings to them helped.

National/International Publications

I made the mistake of thinking that just because I wrote this wonderful book people all over the country would be eager to help me publicize it. This part of the process quickly taught me how important knowing the right people can be. Since I didn't seem to know any of the "right" people, I suffered a lot of grief and headaches trying to get into national publications.

Initially I sent a press release and letter to 35 or so of the most popular mainstream magazines, a few more that I just happened to run across, and a few hundred I got from the *African American Address Book*. It was very frustrating. Every month I would run out to DeLauer's newsstand in Oakland and flip through magazines looking for my mention on their book page, but it was never there. Over nine months of this only once was I pleasantly surprised to see the cover of my book in a magazine — in *YSB* magazine's December/January 1996 issue.

My book has been on several magazine book pages (*YSB*, *Class*, *QBR*, *Esteem*, *Today's Black Woman* and *Black Beat*, bless their hearts)! But I sent to *Essence*, *Vibe*, *Upscale*, *Black Elegance*, *Emerge*, *The Source*, *Rap Pages*, and to more mainstream ones as well, such as

Mademoiselle, Allure, and *Mirabella.* For the first year my book was out I continued to send releases and clips, to no avail. Following up with phone calls might have helped. Especially since my suspicions about knowing the right people was confirmed when I met someone on the internet who worked for a large national magazine and told me that in most cases unless it's from someone they know, most material gets thrown away.

Whether you're in them or not, it's a good idea to keep up on the latest magazines. A wealth of information and potential contacts can be found there. Once, flipping through *Black Elegance* magazine I saw an ad for the Black Women's Expo in Chicago. Through the magazine I got a number for the people in charge and called them to explain that I was a soon-to-be-published author (my book's release was about a month away). The Expo's publicist suggested I fax her my flyer. She took it to a meeting, and a couple of days later I got a packet in the mail from the Today's Black Woman Expo in Chicago-along with an invitation (all expenses paid) to participate! I invited my mother and a few friends to go along and we saturated the expo with *Nappy* flyers. The whole trip was a result of flipping through *Black Elegance* magazine.

I have found articles on and addresses for all sorts of organizations related to Black women (my primary target audience) on the pages of magazines. *Essence* magazine proved to be invaluable. One month they did a story on Black women's support groups and included their addresses. I plugged these into my computer and sent each a letter and flyer to share with their members. I found the Go On Girl! Book club in *Essence* also and did the same for them.

International magazines were really responsive to me and my book. Hanging out at bookstores I ran across two fashion magazines; *Pride*, based in London, and *Panache*, a Caribbean women's magazine. I bought them both and wrote to the editors. My mother happened to be going to London on vacation, so I asked her to hand-deliver a copy of my book to Pride's editor-in-chief at the time Deidre Forbes. It was reviewed in the following issue. My mom was very impressed with Ms. Forbes and the rest of the young Black sisters who worked for *Pride*. Later I sent a bookstore in London a copy of the review to place near my book.

Panache was so enthusiastic they decided to print an excerpt. My chapter on Black women and body image appeared in their section called "Empowering Women." Michelle C. d'Eze, a consulting editor, asked me to write an introduction to the piece and send my signature to them by fax. She thought it would make the piece more personal. The excerpt appeared as a beautiful two-page spread in which they used one of the nude photos of me I mentioned in the chapter. My excerpt was also featured as one of the cover stories.

Pride and *Panache* are only two of many international magazines available in American bookstores. Most of them review books, I'm sure. If any of the others are as supportive as *Pride* and *Panache* were to me, it will be worth your while to get in touch with them.

Local Radio and Television

My first local radio interview was on KSOL, a popular R&B radio station. The public affairs director, a young white woman, wanted to give exposure to local talent. We hit it off and had a great interview. Later I would really appreciate her helping me out the way she did. Though I mailed releases to six or seven other stations with talk shows, the only other one who gave me the time of day was KBLX. I am sure that had a lot to do with Dorothy Reed, the news director whom I mentioned in my book.

Another station who calls itself "the people's station" acted like I didn't exist. The host of one of their popular talk shows said that he would "keep me in mind" when he had a topic related to my book. I wanted to say, "Excuse me, how many other Bay Area 25 year-olds have written and published books? That's a topic in itself." But I didn't. I just waited for him to call, and of course, he never did. Some time later he did a show on images of Black women in the media. Do you think he bothered to call me? Nope. Still, I continued to send him press information each time I mailed to local media.

I did a few local and cable television talk shows as well. I hated doing television, but knew how much it can help get the word out about my book, so I put on my make-up and took the plunge.

Ave helped me land a spot on a popular Black talk show called "Black Renaissance." It is a half-hour show and I had the first segment, a nice fifteen-minute interview. I also did a live, two hour call-in talk show on relationships called "Heartbeat." It is broadcast on a black-owned station called Soul Beat. It also went well and for weeks afterward people came up to me telling me how much they enjoyed the interview.

Television can be unpredictable though. I was approached by a producer about doing an interview for her show, which was geared toward teenagers and young adults. I got really excited, thinking my story would be perfect for them. The TV crew came out to my apartment in December and taped an interview, and the producer told me to call her a few weeks later to find out when it would air. When I did she said it would be in February. So, being the organized person I am, I sent notices to all the schools where I had spoken, telling them that I would appear on this show and to watch for me. I even called a few bookstores and put up signs I made announcing the date and time of the show.

That morning I watched (along with all my family and friends) and during the last five minutes of the show realized my segment was not going to appear on that episode. I was both pissed and embarrassed since I had told so many people to tune in.

I called the producer the next day. She told me they were behind schedule and that my interview would air in April. Said that she would call and let me know the specific date. By the last week of April I had not heard from her so I called again. This time she told me that the show was on hiatus and that my segment wouldn't air until September-nine months after we had taped it! Never mind that I had been telling people for months to watch for me. The show never aired.

The most important part of this story is that even though I was pissed, I managed to refrain from going off on her. There are times when you need to maintain a certain level of professionalism. You should maintain a level of professionalism at all times, but it's especially important during those times when your reputation is at stake.

National Radio and Television

Being interviewed for a syndicated show is the only way I know to get national exposure on the radio. Syndication means that the show will be aired on more than one station. Alvis Davis gave my name to the host of a nationally syndicated talk show called "Today's Black Woman." Even through I did my part of the interview by phone from Oakland, it aired in Coral Springs, Florida. I also did a nationally syndicated radio show with economist Julianne Malveaux. She was really cool but I felt like it was by far my worst interview. Naturally, it was broadcast all over the country.

I made sure to send a letter and newspaper clipping to all of the national television talk show producers. Personally I hate talk shows, but thought if I could get on television and just show the cover of my book, I would be happy. I mailed to about fifteen shows (Oprah, Rolanda and Tempestt included, of course) and to my surprise, got a few invitations!

The Gordon Elliott show called first. They were doing a show on sexism and wanted me to sit on a panel and go head-up with some Israelites. The producers wanted me to fly out that night to appear on the show the next day. Although I had an interesting conversation with one of them, I ended up declining. It just didn't feel right. Some people thought I was crazy, but I didn't care. I didn't want to be on TV hooping and hollering with Black men like the show probably wanted us to do.

The next show to call was The Mark Walberg Show. This particular show was going to be a look back at "the year in racism" and they wanted a young Black woman to sit on the panel. Once again, I had a good conversation with the producer, but they ended up choosing someone else. A few weeks later, at home on Presidents' Day, I saw the show I would have been on if they had picked me. I was glad I didn't do it and thought the woman they chose did a much better job than I would have.

Then, almost two years after *Nappy* came out I got a call from a producer from the Geraldo show. They were doing a show on biracial issues and wanted me to provide "a non-biracial perspective." We talked about my book and position on the topics to be discussed. I had sent them a press release during my Peace of Mind campaign and somehow they ended up with a copy of my book -- perhaps they went out and got it or had my publisher send a copy. In any event, I wondered why it took them two years to call!

I firmly believe that not every opportunity is a good opportunity and I had mixed feelings about appearing on Geraldo. I don't care for Geraldo Rivera and had something a little different in mind for my national television debut, like, for instance, the Oprah Winfrey show! Still, after much contemplation I decided to do it. The idea that one little appearance on a talk show might give me as much publicity and exposure as all the magazines I'd tried to get into (and didn't) made me decide to say yes. I thought about all the people who said they'd seen me on the local cable show-national television meant a million times more! I told the producer I would appear only if they would show the cover of my book. They agreed, so I was off to New York City.

The trip to New York was almost worth the whole experience. I got the royal treatment; they flew me in, had a car pick me up from the airport, put me up in a nice hotel and paid for my meals. I invited my friend Paulette to come down from Boston and she and other friends were able to attend the taping of the show.

I have to say that Geraldo is not exactly the most credible "journalist," if you can even call him that. They had me (and my position on the issues) pegged before

I even opened my mouth. To begin with, they showed a clip from Spike Lee's "Jungle Fever" that was supposed to represent my position on interracial dating. Then at the end of the show they read a quote from my book out of context in an effort to prove that I was saying one thing in my writing and another for the camera. I wasn't given a chance to respond.

By the end of the taping I was upset and not at all happy with how I did. Later I thought to myself, "What did you expect? It's Geraldo." The cover was shown on TV, which was all I really wanted in the first place, and I got a great, free trip to New York.

Many people told me they saw the show. Even I caught it by chance; the producers never notified me when it was going to air. There were ten messages on my machine that day and I got a few letters from people who saw the show and bought my book. One woman from Ohio wrote that she decided to buy the book after hearing Geraldo read from it! Four months later a Black man stopped me on the street and asked me if I wrote a book. He said he saw me on "Geraldo".

My advice is to be careful when doing talk shows. Don't get sucked into the kind of "drama" these shows count on for ratings. Be prepared by thinking of the questions you are most likely to be asked. I don't know what to say about stage fright, only that I wish I hadn't gotten it, or I would have been able to tell Geraldo Rivera where to get off!

Readings and Book Signings

In grade school I was the child who would not ask questions in class because I didn't want everybody looking at me. I hate being the center of attention. It makes me nervous, and more so than most people, I am no good nervous. I tend to forget what the heck I am talking about. During my first television interview I was so nervous that when the interviewer asked me what made me cut my hair off (a question I have answered hundreds of times) I forgot in the middle of my response what I was talking about! It's a big jump to go from being a person who didn't want to speak up in class to being put in front of a camera and asked to pontificate.

Even though I was nervous about reading aloud in public, it never crossed my mind not to do it. I feel like authors sort of owe it people who pay money for our books to read publicly. I know how much I enjoyed hearing authors read from their books, so I decided when the time came reading in public would just have to become one of those fears I took head-on.

I was concerned about reading and which part of my book to read at each event. Glenn, my publisher, told me that I should read one piece all the time until I got it down, and then move on to something else. That was a great suggestion. Because of it, I can probably recite Hair Peace, the first chapter of my book, at the drop of a hat.

My first experience reading in public was at an

evening of poetry and prose called "Our Black Bodies" organized by my great poet friend Marvin K. White. Five Black women were to read, and I was the only one who had never read before. I was scared, but the warmth and support of the audience made it easy and even fun. It also helped that my mother was there, as well as two of my coworkers. The only criticism I received is one I'm still working on: I sometimes read too quickly. Even now I try to slow down my speech when I read.

Most bookstores make flyers to promote upcoming readings and some even place ads in the literary sections of newspapers. Usually they also send announcements to the calendar sections of local papers. Crown Books on Piedmont Avenue in Oakland had my book at the register with a card sticking out announcing that I would be appearing at the store. Still, I never left the responsibility of promoting my book entirely to the store. I would get copies of their flyer for my files and make more copies to give to my family, friends and even strangers with whom I ended up discussing my book.

Since I contacted bookstores myself I was in control of how many events I did and when I did them. One writer I know relies on her publisher to set up her readings. I would never do this! A New York publisher can't possibly know all of the small or independent bookstores in the Bay Area. I always felt more comfortable taking things into my own hands. It also gave me a chance to meet and mingle with the owners and staff of local bookstores. As an author, you definitely want these particular people on your side. When people go into a bookstore and pick up my book, I want whoever is working there to be able to say, "The author of that book is a really great person, and she comes in here a lot, too." Like I said before, a good reputation is invaluable, especially when you are just starting out.

Other Venues

One morning I met a woman at a shopping complex during a local radio station's promotional event. She worked at an elementary school and asked me to speak to her students about being a writer. I was hesitant because they were elementary school students, but went anyway. It turned out to be one of my more rewarding experiences since becoming an author. A month after I spoke at the elementary school one of the students recognized me in the park. The whole thing was incredible and made me realize that even young kids can benefit from my experience.

The next February I was asked to speak at the Black Student Union assembly at a private high school. Because it was Black History Month I had already booked seven or eight other events, I almost said no but when I found out the students would be performing a play written by another student, I knew I had to go. I addressed about a hundred students and their families and friends. It was a true honor.

Putting yourself out there doesn't just mean showing

up where you might sell a book. Once I took a day off from work and spent the morning in a third-grade class, participating in an event called The African American Read Chain. It's an event in which volunteers visit classrooms, read aloud to students, then donate their book to the class. I don't know how the San Francisco School Volunteers got my name but I was happy to participate. I read a different book to the students but told them I was a writer and shared my book with them. I signed one of my head shots for the class and they were thrilled.

It's important to make yourself as visible to the public as possible. Being on television and in magazines is great, but if you are like me and couldn't get a feature story in the paper to save your life, you need to take a grassroots approach.

You will find that you can't please everyone though. One day I was coming out of a restaurant with a friend and in the background heard someone saying, "Hey... Hey..." I ignored it like I always do (hay is for horses, and I don't respond to that.) A guy came up to me and asked if I had been in the Oakland Tribune. When I said yes, he said, "I thought that was you." Then he said something to the effect of, "You should try to be a little more friendly." I explained to him, without getting an attitude, that I don't respond to "hey" and that I had no idea that he had been speaking to me. Told him I was not used to strangers approaching me on the street. He probably left thinking I had major attitude and will go around telling people, "Yeah, I met that young woman who wrote *Nappy* and she was a trip." One week I had three or four people stop me on the street who had seen me at a bookstore or on a cable show. It made me happy, not that I was becoming a "celebrity" but that my Peace of Mind publicity campaign was working -- the word was out about my book.

Burnout
My book came out in May of 1995, and in June, July and August I got busy! Still working at my job, I did eleven readings, the Telegraph Avenue Book Festival, The Black Expo and the African Marketplace in L.A. I was everywhere. It really paid off, but you have to be careful about overextending yourself. You will be no good to anyone if you are sick and tired.

On The Road (Going Out of State)
Since my publisher was a small company and I was a first-time author I didn't get to go on a book tour of several different cities. I figured getting out of the state to promote my book would be left up to me. I was invited to speak at the Central Harlem branch libarary and my publisher agreed to pay for my ticket to New York.

In March of 1996 my full time job ended just in time for me to get on the road to promote the second printing of my book. I decided to spend April and May writing (it had been awhile now since I had done that!) and go on the road in June. Because I had friends in both places, I chose New York and Washington D.C. to start.

After organizing all my readings in the Bay Area, I had no problem figuring out what to do this time. The hard part was trying to get the word out about my events in a city I was not familiar with. I knew from previous experience that I would have to send press releases and events calendars to newspapers, radio stations and television.

All of my events went really well. Since the book had been out for a year, I ran across a few people who had already had the book. It was neat to see my events listed in the local papers. I sent them releases about my events but it is customary for bookstores to do the same thing.

Out in Space: Cyberspace

You'd think I'd be embarrassed about this, but I'm not. I didn't venture out into cyberspace until after my book had been out nine months. It probably would have been longer had I not gotten a call from *American Visions* magazine in Washington, DC, asking me to do an online interview.

I agreed and then almost called back to cancel because I was freaked out about not owning a modem and the fact that I had never been online. I managed to get my act together by the date the interview was scheduled for though and went into the *American Visions* forum. The first thing I saw was this: "Meet Aliona L. Gibson, author of *Nappy: Growing Up Black & Female in America.*" I was blown away! I literally LOLed! (That's cyberspace lingo for "laughed out loud.") It was such a trip. I thought, if this is the first thing people see when they log on to the forum, a lot of people are going to learn about my book.

The interview went really well and ended up going half an hour longer than scheduled. I had a ball. I couldn't quite grasp the concept of being able to chat with people from all over on a scrolling screen, so I asked everyone to tell me where they were from. Milwaukee, Savannah, New York, Washington DC, Houston and Canada were some of the answers. I was amazed. I made lots of "virtual" friends that night -- a grand introduction to cyberspace. For a week after I got electronic messages from people congratulating me on my book and saying they were sorry they had missed the interview.

Basically I learned my way around online services on my own. All of them have different bulletin boards where you can post messages for other people to see. I promptly found the Books & Authors Chat room and posted a message headed "New Author/Nappy". I put one regarding national publications in the Media Chat room and one called "New to Compuserve" in the Meet & Greet room.

Going online has opened up a whole new way for me to get the word out about my book, not only nationally but internationally as well. When you consider that there are other forums on Compuserve, not to mention other services like AOL and Prodigy, the possibilities seem endless.

Additional Printings

Seven or eight months after it's initial release, I got word that my book was to be reprinted — more hardback copies before it went into paperback. I used this as an opportunity to send press releases to announce the second printing. Once again, I sent them to national publications with a book page and the local media. And I will do the same thing when it comes out in paperback! I sent information to all of the people who didn't respond to me the first, second or third time I sent them information. I said in my letter that my book was doing well for a first book, but could do even better with their help.

To the author who has read it aloud a few hundred times it may seem old. But to the public, who may have not heard of you or your book, it isn't. Tina McElroy Ansa's *Ugly Ways* has been on the Blackboard bestseller list for months! Her book came out in 1993 and in late 1995 it was still in *Essence* on the bestseller list.

I had the pleasure of meeting Tina McElroy Ansa at the 35th Anniversary Celebration of Oakland's Marcus Bookstore. She was a warm and wonderful woman. She and her husband Jonee made my heart sing, watching them. She gave me a first edition copy of her book. I also had the pleasure of meeting Paula L. Woods and Felix Liddell, the couple who produced the books *I, Too, Sing America* and *I Hear a Symphony*. They were really wonderful as well. A group picture taken of all of us sits on my coffee table.

It was important for me to meet all of the writers because it dispelled the rumors I had heard about how writers were unfriendly and competitive. Which brings me to the next, very important section.

Networking

As an author it is important to meet and support your peers. You can learn and share information with other writers. Not only that, when it comes time to ask for a blurb (an endorsement) for the back cover of your book, you will have folks to choose from. I can't tell you how many times I have been in a bookstore and noticed someone reading the back cover of my book. Thanks to Evelyn C. White, my writing mentor and good friend, they probably figured my book was the bomb. She hooked me up.

I also met Monique Gilmore, who was so nice and friendly that I invited her to be a co-presenter at a workshop I organized for the the African American Women on Tour Conference. I realized that she could only make my workshop stronger, since we had two different kinds of books out and two different experiences getting published. We complemented each other very well and provided insight and experiences from two totally different perspectives.

Monique and I are now good friends. We learn a lot from each other and support each other as well. I always tell people about her books and she does the same for me. She is a lot more diligent about her writing than I am and that motivates me. Writers need support sometimes in ways only another writer can provide. Monique has really been there for me which has helped me tremendously.

Getting to know other writers is important. It can only benefit you.

The Importance of Saying Thank You

I learned this from my own home training. I was taught to always say thank you to people, to be gracious and show gratitude. Plus, I was genuinely appreciative of anyone who helped me out.

At the end of the year I sent all of the local bookstores thank you notes letting them know how much I appreciated their support. That was one of the most important things I learned from Terrie Williams' book; the importance of saying thank you. I wonder how many other authors take the time to do that? Which ones do you think bookstore people remember most fondly?

Taking The Initiative

I have been called a "model author." I think this is because I have taken it upon myself to get involved in promoting my own work. I cannot stress enough the importance of taking the initiative.

For instance, I decided I needed posters of the cover of my book and instead of waiting for my publisher to send me some, I took a color copy of the draft they sent me and had my own 11"x17" copies made.

Because they were expensive I only got ten at a time, but I kept my receipts and wrote it off as a business expense on taxes. I paid an artist friend of my family's to put foam core on the back of them and distributed them to local stores. I ended up taking twenty to local bookstores. Everyone was really happy to get my posters and I was more than happy to give them to them.

Taking the initiative means going out of your way to promote your own work. I have written so many letters to people and mailed so much stuff they know me at several of the post offices when I go — but I feel like it has paid off. Sometimes in ways that you would not expect. I wrote a letter to the corporate headquarters of The Gap and told them I mentioned them in my book, thanking them for making jeans that work for Black women. I sent a copy of that particular page along with one of my newspaper clippings. I went so far as to suggest that they use me in one of their ads since I have spent (and continue to spend) a lot of money at The Gap. Well, I'm still waiting for that call about the ad, but they did send me a gift certificate for $35 to "encourage the continuing good relationship" between me and their jeans.

Another time I wrote a letter to the book editor at *Ebony* magazine, telling her how impressed I was with their issue dedicated to women but that I was disappointed that my book was not mentioned among the fifty books on their book page. Two issues later, a friend called to tell me that my book was listed on the *Ebony* magazine book page.

Throughout the whole self-promotion process I kept telling myself that my book was not the only one Writers & Readers published that year. I knew they would do something to promote my book, probably send out press releases and review copies, but as I hope you can see from this section, there is much more to it than that! There is no way they could have spent the time or money pushing my book the way I thought it should be pushed. Only I could do that.

The bottom line is this: if you want your book to do well, you have to see to it that it does by taking matters into your own hands. Nobody can or will take the job more seriously than the author. Way back when I was soliciting publishers, I knew that it would be a lot of work but never dreamed that I would go to the extent I did to promote my book. Imagine this, everything I did was in addition to what my publisher was doing for the book!

Closing Remarks

I have learned so much about so many different things since becoming an author. I always kept hearing about how people work harder when in business for themselves than they ever would for someone else. I can second that-since my book has been out I consider myself an entrepreneur of sorts. I spent enough time and money to easily qualify me as such. Spending money on thousands of stamps, getting flyers printed, books, supplies and after I was laid off from my job, copies and faxes, has been a joy for me. I actually enjoy spending money on something I feel so strongly about. I discovered ambition and passion I never even knew existed! Becoming an author has caused me to approach strangers on the street, which was a big deal for me. You will find that you will probably develop all kinds of characteristics you didn't know you had.

By my own standards, my book has been a great success. In the preface of *Nappy* I wrote how initially, I just wanted to "finish something that I started for once in my life". Well, I did way more than that! Getting it published and actually selling copies has made me really pleased with the way things have turned out.

Probably the most important thing I have learned is to follow your own heart and mind. Trust your judgement. I had people who didn't think my book was worthy of being published. I ignored them and did my own thing, thank God. It's hard not to get discouraged sometimes but try to keep your head up and follow your heart. I had several people, agents included, who didn't think this book was a good idea and according to one, I "shouldn't even waste my time doing." Can you imagine? Well, needless to say, I took those words with a grain of salt which is what you have to do sometimes. Obviously, I decided to do the project anyway. I feel good about it and I am happy I have done it. If it helps people, then it will be worth my efforts.

I would love to hear your comments and thoughts on this book, so let me know what you found helpful and what you thought was missing and should have been included. Also, if you are a reference which should be included in the next edition of this book please send me current information including an e-mail address if you have one. Send all letters to:

Aliona L. Gibson
A.L.G. Publishing
2625 Alcatraz Avenue #169
Berkeley, CA 94705

Or call (510) 594-4393!

More Interviews

Q & A with Glenn Thompson, founder & president of Writers and Readers Publishing Inc.

Q: What would you say is the biggest obstacle facing Black publishers today?
A: For existing publishers it would be finances and distribution. The book publishing industry is one that Blacks haven't fully moved into. Book publishing is underfinanced compared to the magazine and music industries. In terms of distribution, more and more Black books are being published, it's getting to a saturation point. The competition is much greater. Large and medium-sized publishing houses are doing Black books, those numbers are going to increase in time.

Q: Do you have any words of wisdom for aspiring authors, people who are looking to get their work out there?
A: The motivation to write and get published has to come from the individual. You will pursue it if you feel passionate about what you are doing. If you are looking at writing like a business, it's a high risk. It can put you and your family in jeopardy, that's the harsh reality.

Q: Is it easier now than say ten years ago for a Black writer to get published?
A: No, it's not easier to get published. There are more possibilities, more choices. More people are buying and more Black books are being published.

Q: Which qualities do you look for in prospective projects?
A: I am here to publish, to do a certain kind of job. I try to

be receptive to instincts, I look for activists and those dealing with freedom, in a very general sense. Freedom of writers to write what they want to write and what they feel like writing. I am interested in activism and see publishing as an opposition. I am in opposition to large publishers or those who just want to publish for money.

Q: Could you give me your general thoughts on the state of Black publishing?
A: What Walter Mosley (author of mystery books including *Devil in a Blue Dress*) is doing is important. (He has signed a contract with a Black publishing company to do his next book). If what he did continues and becomes an example for other well known writers then Black publishing has a future. It is not going to survive if it continues to publish emerging writers and they grow in stature then leave.

We have been kept out for so long. So have our writers and our voices. Only those who are accepted by the liberal parts of white publishing get published.

Q & A with Jacqueline Turner Banks, literary agent

Q. What do you look for in prospective clients?
A. I look for a person who can write, someone who has a good command of the language and somone who understands the importance of good editing. I also look at how a project is presented to me. Presentation is important.

Q. How important would you say an agent is to writers?
A. It really depends on the genre. There is more flexibility in the children's book market. Also new and small presses

use unagented writers.

Q. How do you know how much projects are worth, and what should new authors expect?
A. I do research and find out how much similiar projects have sold for. The quality of the work must be on the same level as what is out there and the work which you have used as a model. An advance of ten thousand or more is a good place to start.

Q. Do you deal with small publishers?
A. I will deal with anyone who will deal with me. If they offer a good advance and the standard royalty percentages I will work with them.

Q. Do you have any words of wisdom for aspiring authors?
A. I am always fascinated by the number of people who don't research or do their homework, for example, sending single-spaced manuscripts filled with typos. Someone recently left a manuscript on my doorstep and it wasn't numbered. That is a real inconvenience. People should not expect agents to tell you how to present your work.

Q. Describe your ideal client?
A. Someone who has something that is ready to go (be presented to prospective publishers) and has done everything possible to make the manuscript saleable. That includes: having a market in mind for your book, knowing if there are similiar books already on the market (if so, who published them), and having contacts in the publishing industry -- this is always helpful. Your manuscript should be picture perfect. The ideal client will also be ready to hand the project over to me and go on with their lives which means starting their next project.

Interview with Reginald Lockett of Juke Box Press, a
poetry publishing cooperative

Reginald Lockett runs a small publishing cooperative
called Juke Box Press. The Oakland based company,
founded in 1978, specializes in poetry and is the oldest of
its kind in the Bay Area. As a cooperative, poets approach
them with ideas or a manuscript and he handles all the
logistics involved in publishing a book, such as the ISBN #,
library of congress card catalog information, typesetting,
printing and book cover design. He also helps writers
research available grants and in some cases pays for projects out his own pocket. The print run of books published
by Juke Box Press varies. For perfect bound he usually does
between five hundred and a thousand books. Chapbooks
are limited editions so he only does between two and five
hundred.

Reginald told me that he thought the advantages of doing
your work with a cooperative is that you control distribution, profit and what goes into the book. He cautions people on the quality. He says you should make sure that all
revisions and editing are done. It should be laid out well,
even the chapbooks. In terms of distribution, as a cooperative he has a company that handles getting the books to
the stores. For chapbooks, he suggests selling them on
your own to independent bookstores. Most chain stores
don't carry chapbooks.

For more information please contact Juke Box Press, 3717
Market St., Oakland, CA 94608

Timeline for "Nappy"

August 1992
Started writing by hand. "Hair Peace" was already written so I started expanding on it.

November 1992
Started inputting it into a computer.

February 1993
Draft One of "Nappy Edges".

March 1993
Wrote synopsis.

May 1993
Started sending out my cover letter and synopsis.

August 1993
Heard from Doubleday Publishing.

June 1993
Heard from Chronicle Books.

October 1993
Heard from Writers and Readers Publishing.

December 1993-April 1994
Edited the book.

February 1994
Signed contract.

July 1994
Received book cover in the mail.

November 1994
Original Publication Date for *Nappy*
(In Fall catalogs as "Nappy Edges").

January 1995
Received a galley of the book.

February-April 1995
Compiled mailing lists, wrote letters of support,
stuffed and labeled envelopes.

April 1995
Mailed 3,000 letters of support and flyers out nationwide.

May 1995
Nappy came out and I had my first book signing
where I sold 44 books in two hours!

April 1996
Book went into second printing.

February 1997
Taped "The Geraldo Rivera Show".

June 1997
My national television debut aired.

Sometime in 1998
Paperback release of *Nappy*!

Glossary of Terms

ABA: American Booksellers Association

advance: money given to an author beforehand by the publisher

agent: a person who sells books to publishers on behalf of authors

anthology: a collection of writings by more than one writer usually with a theme

back order: an order for books which are unavailable and held until book is available

bar code: identification and price marking on a book usually on lower back cover

bibliography: list of books and materials used for a book

bio: brief statement of author's accomplishments and interests

blurb: endorsement printed on back cover of book

calendar of events: listing of events usu. sent out with a press release

chapbook: a small book or pamphlet of poems put out by the poet

clips: writing samples or xerox copies of reviews, articles

contract : legal agreement between author and publisher

copyediting: technical editing: grammar, spelling and punctuation

copyright: legal protection of your work

cover letter: brief letter sent with manuscript

distributor: a company which is responsible for sending books to stores, used by small presses. Large companies have a department

dust jacket: removable jacket cover of hardback books

fiction: novels, short stories, writing based on the author's imagination

first edition: of the original printing or first print run of a book

galley: a typeset version of a book before it goes to the printer

headshot: a black & white publicity photo of an author

imprint: a division of a publishing company, some have several

in print: currently available books

ISBN: International Standard Book Number

Literary Marketplace : a publishing industry directory, the bible of publishing

manuscript: a completed draft of a book before it is typeset

mass market paperback: smaller, cheaper edition of books, usually 4"X6"

news release: (see press release)

non-fiction: autobiography, essays, writings based on facts

out of print: a book no longer available

paperback: a softcover book

pen name: pseudonym used by an author

perfect binding: standard glued on binding of a book

preface: introduction of a book by the author

press kit: collection of publicity materials in a two-pocket folder

press packet: see press kit

press release: announcement giving basic information about an event or your book

psa: public service announcement, release read on the radio

publication date: date book is available for purchase

publicist: a person who handles promotions and publicity

public relations: the field of promotions and publicity

publisher: a company or person who publishes books

query letter: a letter to elicit an interest in one's work

remainders: books left over in a print run

reprint: going back to press or making more copies of a book

returns: books sent back to distribution company or whole saler by bookstores

review: a critical evaluation of a book

review copy: a complimentary copy of a book

royalty: money paid to an author by their publisher

sales rep: a person who presents books to bookstores and wholesalers *self publish:* published by the author

subisidary rights: additional rights of book (book club, film rights etc.)

subsidy press: (see vanity press)

synopsis: summary of book idea

text: main body of a book

trade paperback: quality paperback of a softcover book, usually slightly larger than mass paperback books

unit cost: cost of each book to print

unsolicited manuscript: an unrequested manuscript sent to agent or publisher

vanity press: publisher who charges author to publish their book

wholesaler: a company who buys books for resale to stores

Samples of Work-Related Materials

Original query letter

May 25, 1993

Richard Marek
Editor-at-Large
Crown Publishing Group
201 E.50th Street
New York, N.Y. 10022

Dear Mr. Marek,

I <u>know</u> you've heard about it and you've probably even experienced it personally. I'm speaking of African-American women and our "attitude" problem. Everybody knows that we have a reputation for being mean & nasty and are quick to give you a piece of our mind. The irony is that no one has given much thought to how or why some of us have become that way. With the risk of condoning this type of behavior, I would like to pose a question to you, sort of "food for thought": do you think you would be Ms. Happy-Go-Lucky if you were the product (a citizen, the victim) of a society that was founded on the oppression of people of color (in this case, Blacks) and the suppression of women, a society that promotes the idea that the most "unforgettable women in the world" look nothing like you, and in fact, are the complete opposite of you ?

The collection of writings I am working on will hopefully provide some insight and understanding into why some Black women have an "attitude". "Nappy Edges" discusses the trials and tribulations of growing up Black and female in America and the kind of impact that it has on one's self image. The stories examine and unfold one young woman's quest for self-acceptance and efforts to create her own standards of beauty. This"quest" is an option to living with an inability to appreciate one's own beauty or having an "attitude" (which is a result of low self-esteem and a negative self image) from trying to accommodate the American standards of beauty and in most cases, failing miserably. The stories deal with the issues, events, people and places that have had a direct effect on how she views herself.

"Nappy Edges" is a unique project because it is one of the many voices of a new generation which believes that rap music and "crooning" are not the only forms of creative expression and sharing experiences. The issues at hand are ones that all women will be able to relate to in some way or another. Contrary to popular belief, you don't have to be of the "rich and famous" to have an interesting story to tell. Life is a story and everyone has one to tell, the manner in which it is told is what makes one story more interesting than another.

Enclosed is the information sheet for "Nappy Edges: Growing Up Black and Female in America". If in reading it you are even remotely interested then the finished product will be a "must have" for you.

Thanks for your time,

Aliona Gibson
Aliona Gibson

Book Synopsis

NAPPY EDGES:
Growing up Black & Female in America-
A Collection of Writings by Aliona L. Gibson

Introduction by _____

(guest writer)

"Nappy Edges" is a collection of personal narratives which take a vivid and humorous look at what it's like to grow up Black and female in America. The stories deal with self image and identity and examine the impact of the American standards of beauty on African-American women. Ms. Gibson believes that there is something to be learned from everything we experience in life. Sharing her experiences and writing about them she hopes to encourage others to examine their own experiences. A self-proclaimed "diarist", she is an advocate of using writing as therapy and would like to see more people use this form of creative expression.

Aliona Gibson is a twenty-five year old African-American interested in studying the effects of the media and the American standards of beauty on women of color. She holds a Bachelor of Arts degree from the University of California at Berkeley. Born and raised in Oakland, California, Ms. Gibsons' experiences are sure to both educate and entertain anyone interested in learning about the American experience from an African-American perspective.

Listed below are the stories:

1) **"Hair Peace"** -- Hair is a major commodity in the Black community. Originally written for "Interiors" of Essence magazine, this is an essay that discusses my decision to cut my hair off. This is for anyone who wants to know WHY ??? You'd be surprised how many times I've been asked this question.

1a) **"Hair Peace?"** --This is the sequel to the first part and talks about what happened when I got bored with my short afro. I will talk about my efforts to grow my hair and keep it natural. I will discuss my trials, tribulations and options. I think this piece will be more powerful with visual aides so I will add photos at all the different "hair stages". So "Hair Peace" will actually be a pictorial essay as well.

2) **"Body Language"** --This essay explores my feelings, past and present about my body, from about junior high school to present day. When I was twelve or thirteen I wore a full length wool coat <u>everyday</u>, all day for an entire year. I was bugging big time. I used to hate what I now consider my best physical attributes: hips, booty and being flat-chested. This essay will also explore my decision to be photographed in the nude.

3) **"Going Home"** -- Before my trip to Africa, I had never been out of the state of California. This piece will discuss how a trip I took nearly eight years ago still has a direct effect on my life. I will talk about how the trip changed my life and managed to help create some of my goals.

4) **"Letter to a Friend"** -- In the form of a letter, this piece talks about living in fear of Black men, something I had never experienced before until recently. I experienced quite a few traumatic incidents that made me scared of my brothers.

5) **"Family Portrait"** -- This piece will talk about how my family has had an effect on my self image and identity as a Black person. They think I'm strange.

6) **"The Ultimate Insult"** -- This story talks about how I got dumped for a white girl by a Black man. I will talk about how I responded to this and further discuss the "fever" as it relates to me and also the kind of impact this has on one's self image as a Black woman.

7) **"East vs. West"** -- Having lived in New York for two years, I can now see why people would think California is a strange place. As a native Californian, living in New York I experienced serious "culture shock" I will write about what I think the differences are between the east and west coast.

8) **"School Daze"** - Being educated in predominantly white institutions: Albany, Berkeley and Diablo Valley College has had some kind of effect on the kind of person I am. I will talk about how I think these schools have influenced me. It should be real interesting since I've only ever lived in all Black neighborhoods.

9) **"Undeniably Black"** --This piece talks about what constitutes "beauty" in the Black community and for people of color by American standards and how I fit in, or how I don't fit in I should say.

10) **"Menfolk"** -- This piece pays a tribute to my romantic side. Talks about my preference for Black men and my experiences (both good and bad) with dating. I've decided that this piece will focus on my three "boyfriends" and how they all seemed to last for only eight months. Even though I am an African-American and have had a preference for these men, somehow I do not appeal to them.

11) **"Three Wise Women"** --This is an essay about the three women who are my mentors and have managed to help shape and mold the woman I am. It's interesting because they have a lot in common and they are very different at the same time and I'd like to believe that I am a little bit of each one of them all rolled into one.

My projected date of completion for Nappy Edges is **July 1993**.

Paste-up of Book Review

The Infamous *Nappy* Flyer

Nappy

**by
Aliona L.
Gibson**

**Available February 1995
at bookstores nationwide.**

GROWING UP
BLACK AND FEMALE
IN AMERICA

A personal memoir, *Nappy* takes a vivid and humorous look at what it was like coming of age in the 1980's. The book chronicles how the author came to terms with the politics of identity and how she learned to appreciate her strength and her beauty as a young African-American woman. Topics examined in this autobiographical journey include body-image issues, hair in the black community, interracial dating, and a life-changing trip to Africa.

Aliona L. Gibson, 27, is a native of Oakland, California. She holds a bachelor of arts degree from the University of California, Berkeley. *Nappy: Growing Up Black and Female in America* is her first published work.

Writers and Readers Publishing, Inc. is a black owned company celebrating twenty years of independent publishing. Its list of authors includes some of the most distinguished, award winning contributors to the literary community. *Writers and Readers* "For Beginners" book series has been internationally acclaimed. The company has three imprints: *Writers and Readers, Harlem River Press,* and *Black Butterfly Children's Books.*

General Letter of Support

From the Desk of:
Allona L. Gibson
P.O. Box 5899-169
Berkeley, CA. 94705

February 1995

Hello,

Enclosed please find a copy of a flyer announcing the publication of my book, *Nappy: Growing Up Black & Female in America.*

This flyer comes to you as part of my personal, peace-of-mind publicity campaign. I have spent a countless number of hours working on this campaign. I want to make sure that the word gets out about my book so that it will sell outside of the city where I was born & raised! Please post this flyer or pass it on to someone else who might find it interesting. For those of you who might be really enthusiastic, make copies for your family, friends and co-workers.

Whatever you do to pass the word on will be greatly appreciated.
Thanks for your support.

Sincerely,

Allona L. Gibson

Samples

Events Postcards

Come join us for a celebration reading and book signing for Oakland's own

ALIONA L. GIBSON
AUTHOR OF
NAPPY: GROWING UP BLACK & FEMALE IN AMERICA

HOSTED BY
HEAD DESIGNS

WHEN   SUNDAY, OCTOBER 8, 1995
TIME   3:00 - 6:00 P.M.
WHERE   5038 TELEGRAPH AVENUE
        OAKLAND, CALIFORNIA

Scheduled events for

Nappy:
Growing Up Black & Female in America
by Aliona L. Gibson

Discussion/Booksigning
Barnes & Noble (Jack London Square)
98 Broadway
Thursday, June 22 @ 7:30pm
(Following the Jack London Square Concert Series)
(510) 272-9237

An evening of Poetry & Prose
Walden Pond Books
3316 Grand Avenue, Oakland
Friday, June 23 @ 7pm
(510) 832-4438
*a collaboration with Bay
Area performance poet
Nancy Elizabeth Johnson*

Booksigning
Culture Plus Books
273 Southland Mall, Hayward
Saturday, June 24 @ 3pm
(510) 783-6071

Reading/Discussion
Torchlight Books
353 Grand Avenue (near Perkins)
Sunday, July 2 @ 2-4pm
(510) 272-0737

An Evening of Prose & Poetry
West Berkeley Women's Books
2514 San Pablo Ave. (near Dwight Way)
Friday, July 28 @ 7:30
(510) 204-9399
*a collaboration with
Bay Area Performance Poet
Nancy Elizabeth Johnson*

133

Press Release

**From the Desk of
Allona L. Gibson
P.O. Box 5899-169
Berkeley, CA. 94705**

For Immediate Release
Contact: Allona Gibson
(510) 834-9458

LOCAL AUTHOR PROMOTES HER BOOK, NAPPY: GROWING UP BLACK & FEMALE IN AMERICA IN THE BAY AREA FOR AFRICAN-AMERICAN HISTORY MONTH

Oakland native **Allona L. Gibson**, 28, is the author of a memoir entitled **Nappy: Growing Up Black & Female in America**. After being on the market for seven months, the book is preparing for a **second printing**.

Published by **Writers & Readers Publishing, Inc./Harlem River Press (NY)**, the book deals with issues of self image, identity, and one black woman's quest for self-acceptance. In a personal narrative style, she writes about the politics of hair in the black community, interracial dating, body image issues, life on the east coast, and a life-changing trip to Africa among many other topics. The issues are those which women of <u>all</u> ages will be able to relate to on some level or another

Ms. Gibson has been featured in the Oakland Tribune, The Montclarion, Daily Californian, L.A. Sentinel, YSB Magazine, The Quarterly Black Review of Books and the Washington City Paper among other publications. She has appeared on KBHK's "Black Renaissance", Bay TV Life, TCI Cablevision Alameda and will be featured on KRON's "First Cut" in January 1996.

For more information please call the number listed above.

Letter to Black Women's Support Groups

February 1995

To: A Circle of Sisters
From: Aliona L. Gibson, author **Nappy: Growing Up Black &
Female in America**
Re: Gettin' the word out!!!

Dear Sister,

The time has come. The time for one sister to tell her no-holds
barred, let it all hang out, truth-telling life story (or part of it
anyway). Enclosed is a flyer announcing the publication of my book
which is scheduled to be released next month.

My story is one of self acceptance and self love, two things I think
Black women can never have enough of. *When we love and accept
ourselves it becomes easier to do so for others.* My story is about
putting us on pedestals and understanding that our beauty, as Black
women, is a vast and complex one: we come in a variety of sizes,
shapes & hues with numerous varieties of hair textures and facial
features. In short, my book celebrates our diversity and our beauty.

What I have written is not just "my" story, it's our story. I hope that
every woman of African descent will be able to relate to what I have
written on some level or another. Topics of discussion are those
which I believe transcend age: the hair thang, body-image issues,
male/female relationships and a life-changing trip to Africa, to
name a few.

I found your name in the Circle of Sisters Directory, which is more
valuable to me then all of the other lists I've spent the past five
months compiling!! I believe whole heartedly in the power of "word
of mouth" so I am calling on my sisters to spread the word about
this book. Please copy or post the enclosed flyer. Keep it for yourself
or pass it on to someone else who might be interested. Whatever you
do to help will be greatly appreciated.

I welcome any comments, please contact me: P.O. Box 5899-169,
Berkeley, CA. 94705 Thank you for your time.

Love & Nappiness,

Aliona

Calendar of Events

African-American History Month
events for
Nappy: Growing Up Black & Female in America
(Harlem River Press)
By Aliona L. Gibson

February 1996

Reading/Signing
February 11 (Saturday): Crown Books on Piedmont Ave. (Oakland)
2pm

Reading/Discussion
February 14 (Wednesday): San Jose City College
11am

Reading/Signing
February 17 (Saturday): Barnes & Noble (Jack London Square)
2pm

Reading/Signing
February 18 (Sunday): Nexus Gallery (Berkeley)
2pm

Signing
February 20 (Tuesday): Stacey's Books (San Francisco)
12:30-1:30

Reading/Benefit for Coalition for Ethnic Employees
February 23 (Friday): Center for African & African-American
Art & Culture (San Francisco)
9-11pm

Reading
February 24 (Saturday): Oakland Public Library (Melrose Branch)
48th & Foothill
2pm

Samples

Press Release for Second Printing

From the Desk of
Aliona L. Gibson
P.O. Box 5899-169
Berkeley, CA. 94705

For Immediate Release
Contact: Aliona Gibson
(510) 834-9458

SECOND PRINTING FOR "NAPPY"

*"Aliona Gibson writes like Terry McMillan's Waiting to
Exhale characters talk"*
-Washington City Paper

Nappy: Growing Up Black & Female in America by first time author Aliona L. Gibson is being reprinted eight months after it's initial release.

Published by **Writers & Readers Publishing, Inc./Harlem River Press (NY)**, the book deals with issues of self image, identity, and one black woman's quest for self-acceptance. In a personal narrative style, she writes about the politics of hair in the black community, interracial dating, body image issues, life on the east coast, and a life-changing trip to Africa among many other topics. The issues are those which women of <u>all</u> ages will be able to relate to on some level or another.

Ms. Gibson has been featured in the **Oakland Tribune, The Montclarion, Daily Californian, L.A. Sentinel, YSB Magazine, The Quarterly Black Review of Books** and the **Washington City Paper** among other publications. She has appeared on KBHK's **"Black Renaissance"**, Bay TV Life, TCI Cablevision Alameda and will be featured on KRON's **"First Cut"** in January 1996. She is presenting a workshop called "How to Write, Publish & Market Your First Book" for the **African American Womens Conference on Tour** in March 1996

For more information please call the number listed above.

Letter to Agent

From the Desk of
Altona L. Gibson
P.O. Box 5899-169
Berkeley, CA. 94705
(510) 652-7174

May 21, 1996

Nancy Stauffer
Nancy Stauffer Associates
156-5th Avenue
New York, N.Y. 10010

Dear Ms. Stauffer,

I am a newly published author seeking representation. I have a manuscript for my second book and my third project is in the works. I found your name in the Guide to Literary Agents & Art/Photo Reps.

I have a first draft of a book called "How to Write, Publish & Market Your First Book". The book is a first person account of everything I have learned in my three year odyssey of making my dream of becoming a published author a reality. My book is based on a successful workshop I presented two months ago at the 1996 African American Women on Tour Conference. I have learned a great deal in the past three years and everyone wants to know how I did it, so I think this book will be helpful.

My first book, Nappy: Growing Up Black & Female in America (Harlem River Press, May 1995) has gone into a second printing. I spent six months before it came out organizing my own self promotion campaign which involved handsigning and sending out over three thousand flyers and letters of support. The book sold half of the first print run in it's first two months on the market. It will be released in paperback next year.

If you would like, I can send you my self-produced press packet which includes clips and reviews.

Please let me know if you are interested in working with me. I look forward to hearing from you.

Sincerely,

Altona Gibson

Letter to Black Bookstores

February 1995

To: Black Bookstore Owners & Managers
From: Aliona L. Gibson
Re: **Nappy: Growing Up Black & Female in America** (Writers & Readers, Harlem River Press)

Greetings,

I am writing to introduce myself and to establish what I hope will one day be a long and fruitful rapport. I found your address in either Essence magazine, The Quarterly Black Review of Books or the African American Address Book. Enclosed please find a flyer announcing the publication of my book which is scheduled to be released next month.

I realize that you don't have to be an author to know that Black bookstores can be imperative to the success of books by and about Black people. When asked where they can get my book, I tell folks they can buy it at any major bookstore in the country but I suggest they support our Black bookstores.

My "book hook" is the fact that while numerous memoirs have been written on coming of age as a Black person in this country, with the exception of a few books, my generation hasn't started telling our stories, not in the written word anyway. The first thing people want to know when they've found out that I've authored a book is how old I am, as if you need to be a certain age to feel like you have something to say! A lot of the things I write about in the book are issues for all Black women, regardless of their age. I believe that every woman of African descent will be able to relate to what I have written on some level or another.

For the past five months I've been working on a publicity campaign of my own. As an author, I feel that I need to be an active participant in promoting and getting the word out about my book. I realize that it cannot be done alone which is why I am writing to you. Please post the enclosed flyer and pass the word on about my book. Your support would be greatly appreciated.

Thanks,

Aliona Gibson

Black Literary Agents

Write or call for submission guidelines and always send a self-addressed stamped envelope if you want your stuff returned:

Marie Dutton Brown
Marie Brown & Associates
625 Broadway #902
New York, NY 10012
(212) 533-5534

Faith Childs
Faith Childs Literary Agency
275 West 96th St.
New York, NY 10025
(212) 645-4600

Marlene Connor
Connor Literary Agency
2911 West 71st Street
Richfield, MN 55423
(612) 866-1486

Lawrence Jordan
Lawrence Jordan Literary Agency
250 West 57th St. #1517
New York, NY 10107
(212) 662-7871

Denise L. Stinson
Stinson Literary Agency, Inc.
6632 Telegraph Rd. #327
Bloomfield Hills, MI 48301
(248) 851-7191

Janell Walden Agyeman
(A member of Marie Brown & Associates)
636 NE 72nd Street
Miami, FL 33138
(305) 759-4849

Jacqueline Turner Banks
Banks Communications
7515 Bruno Way
Sacramento, CA 95828
(916) 689-9683

John McGregor
JMG Books
199 Grand Avenue
Freeport, NY 11520
(516) 378-4756

Imar Hutchins
Unable to find contact information

Gay Young
Unable to find contact information

Black Book Publishing Companies

This is just a few publishers. See The African American Address Book and The African American Network (both are listed in "Books") for a more comprehensive listing:

Africa World Press/Red Sea Press
P.O. Box 1892
Trenton, NJ 08607
(609) 771-1666
Contact: Kassahun Checole

African American Images
1909 W. 95th Street
Chicago, IL 60643
(312) 445-0322
Contact: Dr. Jawanza Kunjufu

Black Classic Press
P.O. Box 13414
Baltimore, MD 21203
(410) 358-0980
Contact: Paul Coates

Pines One Publishing
3870 Crenshaw Blvd. #391
Los Angeles, CA 90008
(213) 290-1182
Contact: Denise Pines

Writers and Readers Publishing, Inc.
P.O. Box 461
Village Station
New York, NY 10012
(212) 982-3158
Contact: Glenn Thompson

The Noble Press, Inc.
213 W. Institute Pl. #508
Chicago, IL 60610
Contact: Douglas Seibold

Third World Press
7524 S. Cottage Grove Ave.
Chicago, IL 60619
(312) 651-0700
Contact: Haki Madhabuti

Kitchen Table: Women of Color Press
P.O. Box 908
Latham, NY 12110
(518) 434-2057
Contact: Barbara Smith

Middle Passage Press
5517 Seacrest Drive
Los Angeles, CA 90043
(213) 959-9323

SisterVision: Black Women & Women of Color Press
P.O. Box 217
Station E
Toronto, Ontario M6H-4E2
(416) 595-5033

Just Us Books, Inc.
(specializes in children's books)
356 Glenwood Avenue
East Orange, NJ 07017
(201) 672-7701

Mustard Seed Press
P.O. Box 342
Times Square Station
New York, NY 10108
(718) 443-0257
Contact: Mamadou Chinyelu

Books/Periodicals/Articles

Listed below are helpful books, periodicals and articles:

Books

The African American Address Book
by Tabatha Crayton (Berkley Publishing Group)

*The African American Yellow Pages: A Comprehensive Resource
Guide & Directory*
ed. by Stanton F. Biddle, Ph.D. (Henry Holt)

The African American Network
by Crawford B. Bunkley (Plume/Penguin)

Guide to Literary Agents & Art/Photo Reps
ed. by Kirsten C. Holm
(Writer's Digest Books)

*The Personal Touch: What You Really Need to Succeed in Today's
Fast Paced Business World*
by Terrie Williams (Warner Books)

The Writers Guide to Self Promotion & Publicity
by Elaine Feldman
(Writer's Digest Books)

*The Times of Our Lives: A Guide to Writing
Autobiography & Memoir*
by Mary Jane Moffett (John Daniel & Co.)

The Self Publishing Manual
by Dan Poynter

Literary Market Place-Directory of Publishers
(R.R. Bowker Co.)

On Writing Well
by William Zinsser

How to Write a Book Proposal
by Michael Larsen (Writer's Digest Books)

Bird by Bird - Some Instructions on Writing and Life
by Anne Lamott (Anchor Books)

Wild Mind - Living the Writer's Life
by Natalie Goldberg (Bantam Books)

Writing the Memoir-From Truth to Art
by Judith Barrington (The Eighth Mountain Press)

Periodicals

The Quarterly Black Review of Books
625 Broadway-10th Floor
New York, NY 10012
(212) 475-1010

Your Black Books Guide
912 W. Pembroke Avenue
Hampton, VA 23669
(804) 723-2696

For Black Writers...

B. Ma- *The Sonia Sanchez Literary Review*
P.O. Box 7512
Philadelphia, PA 19104
Contact: F. Elaine DeLancey

Today's Black Woman Radio Show/Newsletter
w/Jennifer Keitt
P.O. Box 9462
Coral Springs, FL 33075
(954) 341-7964

Sisters of the Word
A Newsletter for Black female authors
who write about relationships
Rinard Publishing
P.O. Box 821248
Houston, TX 77282-1248

African Voices
Communications, Inc.
270 W. 96th Street
New York, NY 10025
(212) 865-2982
Contact: Carolyn A. Butts

A Place to Enter
Showcasing Writers of African Descent
1328 Broadway #1054
New York, NY 10001
(212) 714-7032

Shooting Star Review
Black Literary Quarterly
c/o Shooting Star Productions, Inc.
7123 Race St.
Pittsburgh, PA 15208-1424
(412) 731-7464

Writers Digest Magazine
1507 Dana Avenue
Cincinnati, OH 45207

The Writer
120 Boylston St.
Boston, MA 02116
(617) 423-3157

Publishers Weekly
245 W. 17th St.
New York, NY 10011
(212) 645-0027

Poets & Writers Magazine
72 Spring St.
New York, NY 10012
(212) 226-3586

Poetry Calendar, Ince
611 Broadway #905
New York, NY 10012
(212) 260-7092

Our Time Press
290 Grand Avenue #2212
Brooklyn, NY 11238
(718) 622-8093

Women's Review of Books
Wellesley College
Center for Research on Women
Wellesley, MA 02181
(617) 283-2560

For Black Writers...

Articles

"So You Want to Be Published ?"
by Shawn E. Rhea
Black Enterprise Magazine (February 1997)

"Women in Publishing"
Essence Magazine (March 1997)

"Getting Started: A Guide to Writing
Your Own Romance Novel"
by Paula L. Woods
Essence Magazine (July 1997)

"Writing a New Chapter in Book Publishing"
by Carolyn M. Brown
Black Enterprise Magazine (February 1995)

"Publicizing Your Commercially-Published Novel"
by Terry McMillan
Quarterly Black Review of Books (Summer 1994)
Note: Great article for authors of any type of book.

Distribution Companies

(*specializing in Black books)

If you self-publish your book, you might consider contacting a distribution company to carry it. Listed below are a few companies. Call or write for information on how to become part of their inventory. They usually want to know how you plan to promote your book.

*Red Sea Distribution
Lawrenceville, NJ 08648
(609) 844-9583
(800) 789-1898

*Culture Plus Book Distributors
808 N. La Brea
Inglewood, CA 90302
(310) 671-9630

*Frontline Distributors Int'l, Inc.
751 E. 75th St.
Chicago, IL 60619
(312) 651-9888

*Brendon Book Distributors
56 Marietta St. N.W.
Atlanta, GA 30303
(404) 523-3240

*Lushena Book Distributors
1804 W. Irving Park Rd.
Chicago, IL 60613
(312) 975-9945

*A & B Book Distributors
1000 Atlantic Avenue
Brooklyn, NY 11238
(718) 783-7808

*Afro Mission Book Distributors
104 South 13th Street
Philadelphia, PA 19107
(215) 731-1680

Baker & Taylor
P.O. Box 6920
Bridgewater, NJ 08807-0920
(908) 218-0400

Publishers Group West
1700 4th Street
Berkeley, CA 94710
(510) 528-1444

Ingram Book Company
One Ingram Blvd.
P.O. Box 3006
LaVergne, TN 37086
(615) 793-5000

Book People
7900 Edgewater Dr.
Oakland, CA 94621
(510) 632-4700

Small Press Distribution
1341 7th St.
Berkeley, CA 94710
(510) 524-1668

Online/Internet Resources

Please be advised that online addresses and websites
are subject to change!

Black Librarians Discussion List
from the Black Electronic Network
Contact: Listserv@guvm.ccf.georgetown.edu

Genesis Press
Location: http://www.colom.com/genesis
African American romance writers

Multicultural Writers Home Page
Location: World Wide Web
http://users.aol.com/bryantav/
Click: "MWG"

NetNoir Online
Location: American Online/ World Wide Web
Email: davide@NetNoir.com or
http://www.netnoir.com/index.html

Prodigy
Jump: Arts Bulletin Board
Info. on African American books and authors

Callaloo
http://.muse.jhu.edu./journals/callaloo
Original fiction, poetry, art and cultural studies

Fiction Writers Character Chart
http://www.ids.net/~rebecca/character/html

Bookwire www
http://www.bookwire.com/
Lists author tour information book reviews, bestseller list

Romance in Color
www.mindspring.com/~abenson

Website for "The World According to Angela"
Writing tips and chat forum by Black romance writer Angela Benson
(or write P.O. Box 360571, Decatur, GA., 30036)

The Sister Circle Website
www.sistercircle.com

For Black Writers...

AAWOMENLIT@CMUVM.CSV.CMICH.EDU
Electronic mailiing list
(you must have an email address to receive information)
African American Women's Literature

AFAM-L@LISTS.MISSOURI.EDU
Discussions of African American Literature/Criticism

Quarterly Black Review of Books
http://www.bookwire.com/qbr/qbr.html

American Visions Society
http://americanvisions.com

The Griot Online
http://www.afrinet.com

Houston African American Writers Society
http://memebrs.tripod.com/~HAAWS/

American Black Book Writers Association
http://www.blackbookworld.com

Organizations & Agencies

National Association of Black Book Publishers Inc.
P.O. Box 22080
Baltimore, MD 21203
(410) 358-0980

African American Writers Guild
P.O. Box 43874
Columbia Heights, Washington D.C. 20010
(202) 678-8462

American Black Book Writers Association
P.O. Box 10548
Marina Del Rey, CA. 90295
(310) 822-5195

Organization of Women Writers of Africa, Inc.
P.O. Box 652
Village Station
New York, NY 10014
(212) 998-3710
Co-sponsor of Black women writers' conference

Black Literary Club
Black Book Fufillment Club
193 Sterling Place
Brooklyn, NY 11238
Contact: Annette Leach

Black Women in Publishing
P.O. Box 6275
FDR Station
New York, NY 10150
(212) 427-8100

Go On Girl! Bookclub National Headquarters
53 St. Nicholas Place
New York, NY 10031

The Sister Circle
Alexander Book Company
50 Second Street
San Francisco, CA 94105

The Hurston/Wright Foundation
Virginia Commonwealth University
English Department
P.O. Box 842005
Richmond, VA 23284-2005
(804) 828-1331

Bedford-Stuyvesant Reads and Reads and Reads:
A Festival of African Writers, Books and Readers
P.O. Box 342
Times Square Station
New York, NY 10108
(718) 443-0257
Contact: Mamadou Chinyelu

Langston Hughes Community Library & Cultural Center
102-09 Northern Blvd.
Corona, NY 11368
(718) 651-1100
Sponsors annual literary series

Blackboard African American Bestsellers
3354 E. Broad St.
Columbus, OH 43212

Professional Women of Color
P.O. Box 4572
New York, NY 10185
(718) 469-0308
Contact: Monique Brown
Networking organization

African American Women on Tour Conference
3914 Murphy Canyon Rd. #216B
San Diego, CA 92123
(619) 560-2770
Contact: Maria D. Dowd, Founder
Promotional vehicle

African-American Book Club
(Reading Group)
P.O. Box 3196
Berkeley, CA 94703
Contact: Ann Sandifer

New York Public Library
Central Harlem Branch
203 W. 115th St.
New York, NY 10026
(212) 666-9393
Contact: Mr. Leslie Harrison

"Refreshing Minds"
Reading Group
15267 Hesperian Blvd. #306
San Leandro, CA 94578
(510) 357-2367
Contact: Gwen Blackwell

International Association of Black Writers & Artists, Inc.
P.O. Box 43576
Los Angeles, CA 90043
(213) 964-3721

Zica Creative Arts & Literary Guild
1790 60th Avenue
Sacramento, CA 95822
(916) 422-0820
Contact: Ethel Mack-Ballard

African Eye Cultural & Educational Programs
2134 Wisconsin Avenue
Washington, D.C. 20007
(202) 338-6200
Contact: Virginia Bullock

A Circle of Sisters: Conscious Connection
c/o Hafeezah Basir
The Unlimited Self
405 W.147th Street
New York, NY 10031
Directory of sister support groups

National Writers Union
UAW Local 1981
East Coast: 113 University Pl. 6th Flr., New York, NY 10003
(212) 254-0279
West Coast: 337-17th St. #101, Oakland, CA 94612
(510) 839-0110

International Women's Writing Guild
Box 810 Gracie Station
New York, NY 10028
(212) 737-7536
Contact: Hannelore Hahn

California Lawyers for the Arts
Ft. Mason Center
Bldg. C, Room 255
San Francisco, CA 94123
(415) 775-7200

Library of Congress (Form TX.)
Register of Copyrights
Library of Congress
Washington, DC 20559
(202) 707-3000

ABI Department
R.R. Bowker Company
121 Chanlon Rd.
New Providence, NJ 07974
(800) 521-8110
For forms to be listed in Books in Print

ISBN U.S. Agency
R. R. Bowker
121 Chanlon Rd.
New Providence, NJ 07974
(908) 665-6770
For information on ISBN numbers

American Booksellers Association
560 White Plains Rd.
Tarrytown, NY 10591
(800) 637-0037
For information on the annual ABA convention

Pen Center USA West
672 Lafayette Park Place #41
Los Angeles, CA 90057
(213) 365-8500

Association of Authors' Representatives, Inc.
10 Astor Place, 3rd Flr.
New York, NY 10003
(212) 353-3709
List of member agents

For Black Writers...

Workshops/Retreats/Conferences

Hurston/Wright Writing Retreat
c/o Hurston/Wright Foundation
Department of English
Virginia Commonwealth University
P.O. Box 842005
Richmond, VA 23284-2005

National Black Writers Conference
c/o Medgar Evers College, C.U.N.Y.
LLCP Department
1650 Bedford Avenue
Brooklyn, NY 11225
(718) 270-5049

Mothertongue Institute for Creative Development
P.O. Box 16217
Oakland, CA 94610
(510) 273-2463
Contact: Aya de León

Flight of the Mind
Women's Writing Retreat
622 Southeast 29th Ave.
Portland, OR 97214
(503) 236-9862
Contact: Judith Barrington
Please send self-addressed stamped envelope.

Soapstone- A Writing Retreat for Women
Same info. as Flight of the Mind

Cottages at Hedgebrook- A Retreat for Women Writers
2197 E. Millman Rd.
Langley, WA 98260
(360) 321-4786

Norcroft- A Writing Retreat for Women
32 East First St. #330
Duluth, MN 55802
(218) 727-5199

The Writer's Voice
5 W. 63rd Street
New York, NY 10023
(212) 875-4124

Djerassi Residency Artists Programs
2325 Bear Gulch Road
Woodside, CA 94062
(650) 747-1250

Yaddo Colony
P.O. Box 395
Union Avenue
Saratoga Springs, NY 12866
(518) 584-0746

Mac Dowell Artist Colony
100 High Street
Peterborough, NH 03458-2485
(603) 924-3886

Chicago State University's Annual Black Writer's Conference
c/o Gwendolyn Brooks Center for
Black Literature and Creative Writing
9501 South King Drive
Chicago, Il 60628
(773) 995-4440

Cave Canem -- Retreat for Black Poets
c/o Toi Derricotte
166 N. Dithridge Street #3E
Pittsburgh, PA 15213

For Black Writers...